How To Play From A Fake Book

by Michael Esterowitz

Book Design by Richard Deon

Table of Contents

What Is a Fake Book, and Why This Book?

1

A "fake book" is a collection of music—usually popular, traditional, ethnic and semi-classical tunes—arranged in skeletal form providing just the melody and the symbols for the accompanying chords. (They are presented in as abbreviated form as possible, with repetitions of sections and even slight variations not written out in full.) The actual playing of the song with full accompaniment is meant to be improvised or "faked" by the performer.

For years, fake books were used mostly by professional musicians, such as cocktail pianists or those in wedding or society bands. These books were invaluable to them because the condensed manner in which the music was presented allowed a lot of songs (up to 1000 or more!) to be published in one volume. Also, sightreading a song for the first time is usually a lot easier from a fake chart than from a full piano score, the latter having many more notes to read and pages to turn. They also give "pros" the freedom to stylize a song their own way, rather than to play it as arranged in a sheet music version.

The older "pro" fake books were usually not available to the general public. They could not be sold "over the counter" in music stores because they were illegal. (Their publishers did not pay royalties or secure permission to reprint the tunes from the rightful owners; hence, they broke copyright laws designed to protect composers.) Probably because of their underground or "bootleg" status, these illegal fake books often tended to be sloppily edited, mistake-ridden and difficult to read.

In recent years, however, "legal" fake books intended for amateur and professional musicians alike have become available. Players attracted to the obvious economy of these fake books have been buying them, but unless one knows how to use them, the results will not be satisfying.

Just what does one need to know to play from a fake book? For one thing, how to read simple music notation. This ability is assumed here. Although fake books only print music in the treble clef, our musical examples of how such renditions might be carried out are written in full piano scores.

There are two other things we need to learn to play successfully from a fake book. One is how to interpret chord symbols—that is, how to actually play all the various types of chords you will run across. This is not such difficult information to learn. Music tends to be fairly logical and consistent, and a chord type in one key will work the same way in another key. There are, in addition, common chord progressions (chord "changes," in musicians' jargon) which will help us make sense of most of the music we encounter.

The other main thing we need to learn is how to make the accompaniment interesting—how to give some character to the chords and rhythms in order to add flavor and motion to our playing. Merely fingering the correct notes of each chord is often not really satisfying—the total effect may be dull and amateurish. Yet *it doesn't take all the skill and dexterity of an advanced pianist to sound professional.* It's amazing how pleasing the results can be using quite easy-to-play patterns.

This book will focus on those different accompaniment patterns, and on how to play any tune in a stylistically correct way. By the time you finish it, you should be able to play any song in any fake book in a style fitting the tune. More advanced subjects, such as jazz improvisation ("taking off" on a tune) will only be lightly touched on, but hopefully this book will be a good start for pianists who wish to go on to those other areas.

Unless you are one of those very rare people who can play completely by ear, some knowledge of music theory is necessary in order to be liberated from having to read all the notes of a piano score. This book will provide you with a short study of theory. However, we will go slowly and present lots of musical examples, so things will be clear and fun, even for those of you who thought understanding Einstein's Theory of Relativity was a prerequisite for music theory!

Intervals and Scales

2

All the music we will play has three main elements: the melody, the harmony and the rhythm. The basic melody is given to us in a fake chart (which later we may wish to adorn and embellish). The rhythm and the harmony of the accompaniment are the elements we have to provide (guided by the chord symbols given and the style desired). Before we begin forming chords or discussing styles, let's spend a little time on some of the building blocks of music, because it is from these that we will learn to create our harmonic accompaniments.

Intervals

An interval, put most simply, is the distance between two notes. Most good melodies contain a variety of intervals; that is, the distance and the direction (up or down) between succeeding notes will vary.

For instance, let's take the melody from the folk song "Blue Tail Fly" and look at the intervals involved.

Notice there are some repeating notes, but there are also movements up or down of different distances. How do we label these distances? Intervals are given numbers which define their distance. If we start on the first note and count up or down the lines and spaces of the staff until we reach the second note, the total number (counting our starting note as one) is the interval. In the melody above, the first note is D, which moves to G. Including our starting note, we can count up four notes — D, E, F, G — so this interval is a *fourth* up. The G, after repeating twice, moves to F#. Counting G as one, we count to two, so this interval is a *second* down. This is followed by a *third* up, (F#-A) and a *fifth* down (A-D). On your own, fill in the rest of the intervals for this melody.

Larger intervals which don't appear in the above tune include the sixth, the seventh, and finally the octave (from the Latin word for eight), which occurs when the same note is repeated at the next higher or lower level. Intervals beyond an octave are called *compound* intervals. The largest interval we will refer to is a thirteenth.

Intervals within an octave range from a second (two notes that are the same would be called a unison) to a seventh. Yet, if we count the number of keys within an octave, we know we have twelve. How can seven interval numbers account for twelve notes? The answer is that intervals can have different qualities. For example, all of these are fifths:

We'll look more closely at the different qualities that intervals can have a little later on. For now, let's go over some familiar melodies and see what intervals they are made of. Below are the opening measures of the national anthem. The intervals of the first phrase are already identified. Fill in the remaining ones.

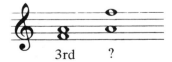

Notice that the most common intervals are seconds. This is the case with most good melodies; when the melody proceeds by seconds, it is said to be moving *step-wise*. (Too much step-wise movement will tend to get boring.) Compound intervals in vocal melodies are rare because of their awkwardness for singing, but they are important in harmony, which we will get to later. Here is another familiar melody which does use compound intervals. Again, fill in the missing intervals on your own.

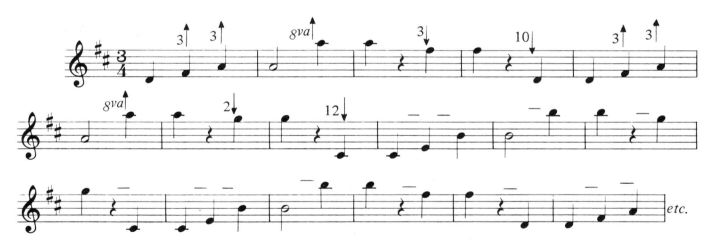

Now let's try something else with intervals. What happens if you "flip-flop" them? Take the third F to A. If you take the F and move it up an octave (or take the A down an octave), what happens to the interval?

If you answered that it becomes a sixth, you were right. Notice the sum of the two intervals (3rd + 6th) is nine. Try this with other intervals (up to an octave), and the same thing will happen. Such flip-flopping is called *inversion* and will prove to be a very important concept when we build our chords.

Triads (Part 1)—The Major Chord

3

An interval is formed by playing two different notes (either simultaneously, which is a *harmonic* interval, or in succession, which is a *melodic* interval). A *chord* is formed by playing *three* or more notes *simultaneously.* *Harmony* refers to how these chords are built (the combinations of intervals), and how they move from one to the other. Actually, the notes of a chord don't have to be literally simultaneous; they can be broken in time as long as our ears group them together.

The simplest three note chords are called triads. At the bottom of a triad is the *root* note, the note for which the chord is named. The other two notes of a triad lie respectively a *third* and a *fifth* above the root. A good way to remember this is to assign the root note of the triad the number 1, the middle the number 3, and the top note the number 5.

As was mentioned earlier, these intervals can have different qualities, and so any of the triads to the left are possible with a C root:

The first chord we will work with is the major triad. We can find it easily by playing a C major scale:

Taking notes 1, 3 and 5 of the scale produces a C major chord!

The interval between notes 1 and 3 here is known as a "major third." (You can find a major third beginning on any note by counting up or down two whole steps. The shortest distance between two notes is a half-step — C to C# or E to F, for example. Counting from C to E we'll find four half-steps, which equals two whole steps.)

The interval between notes 1 and 5 in the major triad is known as a "perfect fifth." (A perfect fifth may be found by counting three-and-a-half steps.)

Let's try a little test for your ears. Take the seven notes of the C major scale and build a triad on each note, using only the notes in the scale. In other words, your first chord will be scale notes 1, 3 and 5 (C-E-G); the second chord notes 2, 4 and 6 (D-F-A); the third chord notes 3, 5 and 7 (E-G-B), and so on. Now, how many of the chords you just played were major, and on which scale notes (roots) did they appear? If you answered three (on the first, fourth and fifth scale notes), you were absolutely correct! To have made any of the other scale notes serve as the root of a major triad would have required the use of accidentals. If you try the same thing in any other major scale you will get the same result — major chords appear "naturally" on the first, fourth and fifth notes of a major scale. Here is a demonstration in C and G.

Notice that we have used Roman numerals to refer to the scale tones on which the chord is formed. This is common musical practice, and a habit that will be beneficial for you to develop. It will help you understand harmonic relationships in music, which is indispensable if you want to transpose. While fake charts themselves never use these Roman numeral designations (they use actual chord names), the more we understand how harmony is put together, the better our overall musicianship will become!

The three major triads (the I, IV and V chords of any given key) are the most common chords, be it in folk music, classical, rock, blues, etc. (They are sometimes given the special names of the tonic [I], the dominant [V], and the subdominant [IV].) Literally countless songs are harmonized by just these three; among them are such traditional and folk songs like "Oh, Susanna," "Glory, Glory, Hallelujah," "This Land is Your Land," "The Marine Song," "Red River Valley," "He's Got the Whole World in His Hands" and "Yankee Doodle."

Since many songs are played in simple keys such as C or G, by learning just a few major triads we can play a whole set of tunes right away! In C major, our three basic chords are C (I), F (IV) and G (V). In their simplest form in the left hand these chords will be played as follows:

Let's try these chords right away with a fake book version of a tune we all know. Simply play the chord written above the staff in the left hand, repeating it on the second beat of each measure (as indicated by the arrow). The right hand has to play only the melody as written.

That was easy, wasn't it? You are on your way to becoming a good faker! You should now begin to practice playing major triads on all twelve roots. (Note: the symbol 𝄪 indicates a double sharp. It is ½-step higher than a sharped note.)

Note: 𝄪 = double sharp (note raised 2 tones)

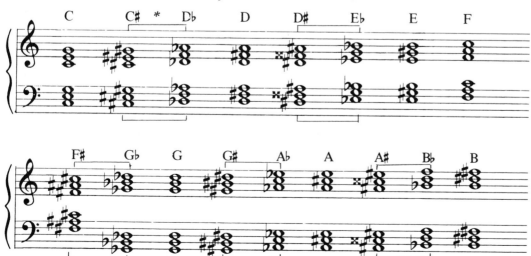

bracketed chords are enharmonically related. Same pitch, different names.

Using only the major triads, we can now begin to read and study some fake arrangements. At first, we will do this in the most elementary form, with the melody played by the right hand and the chord accompaniment by the left. (Note that a chord letter with nothing following it means major triad; the actual word "major" is not necessary. If no new chord is provided above a measure, the last given chord is retained until a change is indicated.)

For each tune or example we present in this book, we will suggest a possible rendition or "realization" for purposes of study. These suggested realizations are not to be construed as the definitive way to play these tunes, but are there merely to provide appropriate examples to learn from. (The word "realization" was a term used in the seventeenth and eighteenth centuries to refer to how a player would carry out the "fake charts" of that time — the so-called "figured bass." Faking an accompaniment has a long and noble history in "serious" music, not just in popular styles!)

Below is a familiar folk song, "On Top of Old Smoky" (in C) in fake book form. Try to work it out on your own, playing all the notes of each chord together in the left hand at the beginning of each measure, holding them down for the entire measure. Play the chords in the octave starting on C below middle C — if you play them in the next lower octave they will be muddy sounding. Your realization will come out like this:

The chords are all correct, but, admittedly, this is not a very interesting arrangement. Why not? Because there is no movement in the accompaniment; the chords just "plop" down and stay put. In other words, there is nothing happening rhythmically. What can we do to make things more interesting? This brings us to our next chapter.

Basic Accompaniment Patterns (or "What Can I Do With My Left Hand Right Away To Sound Good?")

Without a pulse or a beat, music would be lifeless. You probably know that each measure of music is divided into beats, usually two, three or four, called duple, triple or quadruple meters, respectively (or multiples of them in the case of compound meters). The downbeat (first beat) of the measure is always strong or slightly accented, and is followed by a weak beat. A duple (2) or quadruple (4) meter will have a pattern of strong-weak or strong-weak-moderately strong-weak, respectively, while a triple meter will sound strong-weak-weak. If we can play our accompanying chords in a way that strengthens this basic pulse, we will have gone a long way towards making our music more attractive.

Let's stay with "On Top of Old Smoky," which is in triple meter. Try breaking up the chords so that the root note is played on the downbeat while the remaining two notes of the triad are played together on the weak second and third beats of each measure. Since the root is on the lowest bass note of the accompaniment, it automatically sounds a bit stronger than the higher notes; this helps bring out the strong beat pattern. (Our ears are always able to pick out the lowest and highest notes most readily.) This "broken chord" accompaniment in a ¾ meter is our most basic waltz-type left hand pattern. (Note that the numbers below the chords refer to chord tones and not fingering.)

A variation of this (which is fuller but a bit harder to play) is to strike the root note on the downbeat an octave lower, followed by the full triad. This gives it a real "oom-pah-pah" sound.

For added emphasis you could double the bass in octaves:

Another basic accompaniment is to *arpeggiate* the chord, that is, to play it one note at a time. (Actually, if we use the piano's sustain pedal we can hear the separate notes of an arpeggiated chord together. This is one reason why good *careful* use of the pedal can often help flesh out the accompaniment.)

Here is a way to arpeggiate our "Old Smoky" chords:

Chord tones:

This means play the same as previously written.

When arpeggiating a chord, we don't have to always play the notes in the same order. For instance, try playing the fifth of the triad on the second beat and the third of the triad on the last beat.

Chord tones:

Let's try another song, this time using a different key and meter. Here is "Jingle Bells" in fake book form, followed by a realization with simple "block chords" appearing two per measure.

Again, pretty dull stuff. Let's again try breaking up the chords. This time we have to alternate every other beat since we are in 4/4 time.

As we did before, we can vary this by lowering the root bass note an octave and playing the full triad on the second and fourth beats. Similarly, we can easily double the root an octave higher in the bass if we wish.

This certainly sounds better than just playing the "block" triad and holding it down through each measure, but the repetition of the bass notes can get pretty tiresome, too. Let's see how we can further vary this.

One very common and effective accompaniment pattern in quadruple (4) meter is to have the bass alternate between the root and fifth of the chord on the strong beats. The rest of the chord is played on the two weak beats (beats 2 and 4). By alternating bass notes we avoid the annoying static quality of hitting the root of the chord continuously. Below is the "1-5" bass pattern for our "Jingle Bells" chords:

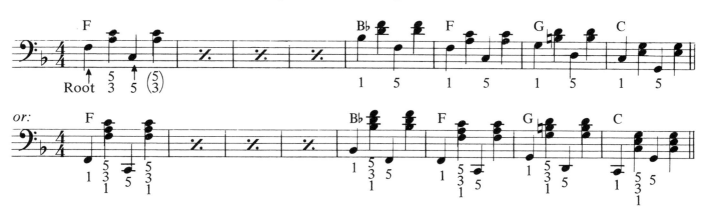

In order to arpeggiate the chords in this 4/4 meter, we obviously must repeat one note of the chord (assuming we are playing triads at the rate of one note per beat) in each measure, since the chord has only three notes. This can be done in a variety of ways:

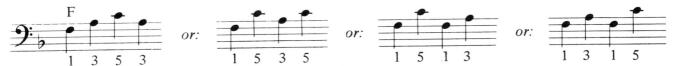

If we want to get a bit fancier and double the root note of the chord an octave higher, then our possibilities increase.

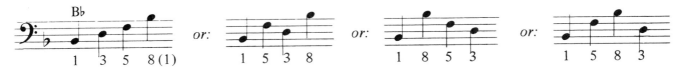

These are some basic accompaniment patterns that you can use right away. We will continue to use them while we expand our knowledge of chords. Let's now learn the other basic triads; this will greatly increase the number of songs we will be able to play.

Triads (Part 2) – The Minor Chord

5

Now that we've discussed basic accompaniment patterns for major chords, it's easy to use the same ideas for the other triad types. Let's start with the next most common triad, the minor triad.

The only difference between the minor triad and the major triad is that, in the minor version, the middle note, the third, is flatted to its closest lower neighbor. Counting by steps on the keyboard, this means 1½ steps between the root and the third (making a "minor third"), and two whole steps between the third and the fifth. Let's look at a C minor triad as we would see it on both a staff and a keyboard.

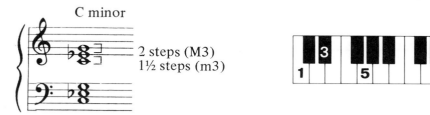

2 steps (M3)
1½ steps (m3)

Note that the proper spelling of a C minor triad is C-E*b*-G, not C-D#-G. Remember that the spelling of a chord has to indicate the intervals between the notes.

By knowing only a few minor chords, we enormously increase our potential repertoire of songs. For instance, here are the left hand root positions for A minor and D minor.

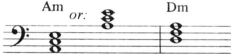

With just these two chords added to a C or a G major chord, we can play many standard 1950's-type chord patterns, such as the one appearing in "Heart and Soul". Try the melody below, inserting the chords on each quarter note so that every chord gets played twice. We've started it for you.

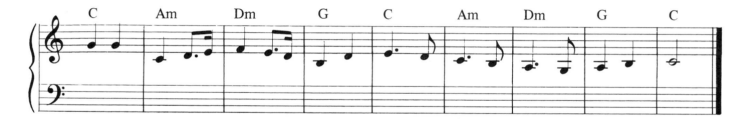

15

To tell the truth, this pattern is a little unexciting. Let's break up the harmony between the bass note and the rest of the chord as we did previously, but with a slight variation. Instead of bass-chord-bass-chord, let's try bass-bass-chord-chord (using eighth notes, because we are in 2/4 time).

Now try the same ear test on yourself as you did for major chords. Go up a major scale (C is OK), building a triad rooted on each scale tone. How many chords of the seven were minor and on which scale numbers did they occur? The answer is three (same as major), built on the second, third and sixth scale tones. Below is a demonstration in G, again using Roman numerals. (Some musicians like to use lower case Roman numerals for minor chords, to distinguish them from majors.)

As we did for the major triads, we can now build a minor triad on all twelve root notes.

Let us now look at a fake book arrangement of a tune using minor triads. Several different symbols are used to indicate minor chords. The most common is a small "m" or "min" following the chord letter, but sometimes a minus sign is used, as in A-. The first tune we will look at, "Hatikvoh," is in E minor, and uses two minor chords (on the i and iv of that key). Let's try it first with the triads blocked out in their simplest form in the left hand, with the right hand playing the melody.

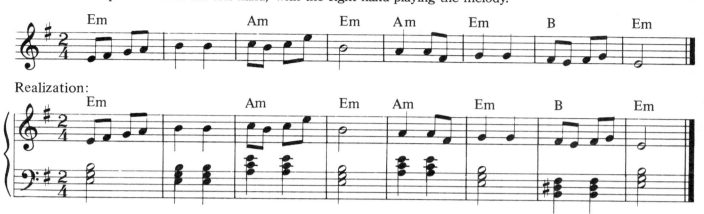

Realization:

Of course this is too static to be a good arrangement. Let's again apply our principle of alternating bass notes on strong beats with the rest of the chord (or the full chord) on weak beats.

or:

or:

You can also try alternating the root and the fifth of the E minor chord for the opening two measures. This would give you the fifth of the chord on the down beat of measure 2, which sounds OK because the root of the chord was already well established in the first measure. An arpeggio chord pattern could also be used:

All these patterns sound a lot better than just banging out block chords, but is there anything else we can do to help fill out our basic arrangement? Until now, we have used the right hand to play only the melody. The right hand can contribute more than this, which brings us to our next chapter.

Fleshing Out the Harmony (or, "What Else Can My Right Hand Do Besides Play the Melody?")

6

The left hand contributes most of the rhythmic character to our arrangements. Sometimes this requires that it not play a complete harmony; it may, in fact, play only one note at a time. However, the right hand can "help out" with the harmony while it is playing the melody.

Look again at the tune we just worked on, "Hatikvoh." Let's try adding one or two harmony notes to our right hand part to help fill out the space between the melody line (on top) and the left hand accompaniment (on bottom).

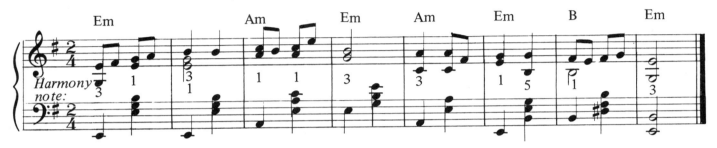

Notice that we didn't add a harmony note to coincide with every melody note. This would make the texture too thick; it would also be more awkward to play. The harmony notes are played on the strong beats at the beginning of each measure and sometimes again on the second strong beat. (Whether the added harmony note[s] should be held down throughout the measure or released instantly is determined by the placement and position of those notes, and by the sound desired. Use of the sustain pedal can eliminate the need for our fingers to hold down the harmony notes, but be careful of over-pedaling!)

The number of harmony notes added below the melody obviously affects how thick the sound will be. The right hand might play three notes at a time (the melody note doubled an octave lower by the thumb with the other two chord notes in between). You may notice that this can put the notes of the chord in a different order than we've previously seen. The ability of a chord to be played in different note orders is very important; this concept will be developed later.

For now it will be easiest for you to use just one harmony note under the melody in the right hand. How do you know which note to use? One possibility is to play the closest chord tone just below the melody note. Sometimes, when the melody has a descending line, this doesn't work so well, because the melody tends to run into the harmony. In those cases it's more comfortable to use a harmony note farther from the melody line. For instance, look at the melody fragment below, played twice with an E minor chord harmonizing it.

In the first example the fifth of the E minor chord, B, is used under the melody in the right hand. Because the melody "walks down" to B, we have to let go of the harmony B to play it again as a melody note. This is perfectly all right, but it's smoother to use the third of the chord, G, as the harmony note, as we do in the second example. This way we can keep it held down throughout the measure.

When adding right hand harmony notes, an important thing to be aware of is which chord tones are missing from the left hand. If we are playing an arpeggio, or an alternating note-chord pattern in the left hand, the chord may not be identifiable right away unless the melody itself fills in the missing harmonic "gaps". For instance, in our suggested right hand part for "Hatikvoh", we add a G harmony note — the third of the E minor chord — below the melody on the very first downbeat. Since the left hand may only be playing the single root note E, the G helps establish the minor quality of the chord right away. (Remember, the third of the chord is what distinguishes major from minor triads.) It is not necessary to play all the notes of a chord on the very first beat, but it is generally important that the third of a chord be included, in order to have a full chord.

For practice, go back to all the tunes previously presented and add harmony notes in the right hand, keeping the same left hand accompaniments used before.

Triads (Part 3)
Diminished and Augmented Chords

7

We can now complete the remaining two triad types and apply them to various songs.

Diminished Triads

Have you ever wondered how those silent movie accompanists create all that tension and excitement during a suspenseful scene? Easy! Just learn to play a series of diminished chords and you can have all your listeners wondering if the hero will be able to untie his sweetheart from the tracks before the train runs her over!

Of course, this is an exaggerated (and cliched) use of diminished chords, but it demonstrates how they convey an unresolved sound. Let's see why.

Whereas major and minor triads can convey the "home key" or resting place of a tune, diminished triads must always lead somewhere else. They are unsettled. Like the major and minor triads, diminished triads have roots, thirds and fifths, but *both* intervals are minor thirds, or 1½ steps each. Therefore, the fifth of the chord ends up half a step short of a perfect fifth; it is a *diminished fifth*. Let's play a C diminished chord.

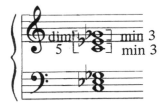
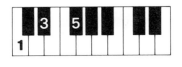

If we go up a major scale and build natural triads on each scale tone, as we did before, which scale number will form a diminished triad? This is easy, because there's only one scale number left, the VII chord. In C major, this would be a B diminished chord, as shown below. This completes all the "diatonic" triads—those which can be built on the seven tones of the major scale without adding any accidentals. (Chords that do have such alterations are called "chromatic.")

I   ii   iii   IV   V   vi   vii°   I

Diminished chords are usually indicated in fake charts by the abbreviation "dim" after the chord letter, or simply by a little circle, as in A°. Let's now construct diminished triads on all twelve possible roots.

Diminished triads

Because of their "just passing through" quality, diminished chords are rarely lingered over the way major and minor chords are (except when one deliberately builds tension, as in our "silent movie" music).

Let's look at a fake book arrangement of a tune using the three triads we have learned so far.

Notice that our suggested realization uses an arpeggio pattern playing each chord note separately. This works well to create a delicate "classical" effect; it is not as rhythmic as the bass-chord-chord 3/4 (waltz) pattern seen earlier. (Work out both ways to hear the difference. Which do you prefer?)

Once you get a left hand pattern down fairly well, start adding right hand harmony notes to your arrangement as well.

Augmented Triads

All of us have heard a "torch singer" about to start a steamy ballad when her pianist/accompanist leads her in with a single long rolled-out chord that right away somehow conveys the proper mood of longing and mystery. What is that somewhat strange but certainly not disagreeable or harsh chord? Often it is an arpeggiated augmented chord.

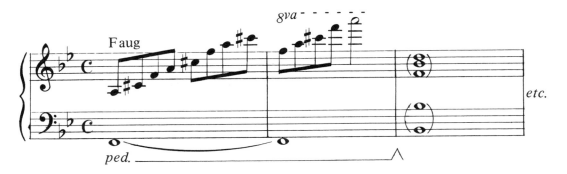

In contrast to the diminished triad (which is composed of two consecutive minor thirds), the augmented triad consists of two consecutive major thirds. The "augmentation" refers to the fifth, which is sharped a half-step higher than the fifth of a normal major triad. The augmented chord has a spicy unresolved sound that is generally used sparingly. Sometimes it appears as part of a series of chords in which one "voice" is moving while the other chord tones are staying still. We'll see examples of this later.

Forming a C augmented chord on our schematic keyboard, we count up two whole steps from our root note C to the third E, and another two whole steps from E to G#.

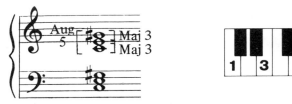

Now let's form augmented triads on all the other roots:

Fake charts indicate augmented chords by the abbreviation "aug" after the chord letter, or by the symbol "+". Occasionally a "#5" might be used, since this indicates which chord tone is altered in order to get an augmented sound.

You only have to learn four different combinations of notes on the keyboard to be able to play all the augmented chords. Augmented chords built on C, E and G#, for example, share the same notes. The same is true for C#, F and A.

Let's try a fake book arrangement of a tune using all four triad types.

Try to work out your arrangement in steps. First, block out the left hand in full triads. Then add the octave on top with the thumb.

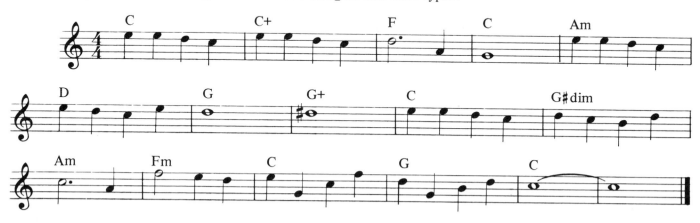

Next, break up the left hand chord separating the bass and the rest of the chord to establish a rhythmic pattern.

You can also try arpeggiating the chord. Below you'll find a different arpeggio pattern for each of the first three measures.

When you have that down well for the entire tune, try to add some harmony notes under the melody in the right hand.

Once all that is comfortable, try some other variations. First, use different rhythms in the left hand, such as below.

Make up some other rhythmic variations on your own. If you use other rhythm values (such as eighth notes and dotted notes) you can get as complex as you wish. Obviously, more complex accompaniment rhythms add more difficulty to the coordination of the hands. (Independent practicing of the hands is very beneficial.)

The final step would be to combine different patterns in one performance. Below is such a possibility worked out in full.

Inversions (Part 1)

Let's take the little tune we just worked on and try a new twist. Suppose we take the left hand chords and "flip-flop" them so that they come out in a different order of notes. In other words, the bottom note of the chord will change:

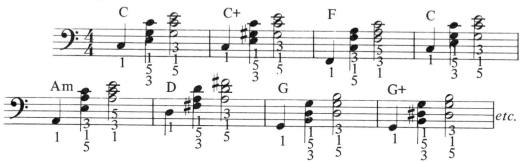

In the first measure we will strike the root of the C chord, followed by the rest of the chord (E, G and C restated an octave higher). Then we'll change the order of the chord, moving it "up a notch" to G, C and E. A chord retains its basic quality *no matter what order its notes are played in.* This is called "inverting," and the different chord forms are called *inversions.*

In the above example, we see that once we strike the bass note on the root of the chord, we can play the follow-up chord in any order. The use of inversions in this example provides a little movement in the left hand accompaniment. This freedom to invert chords helps us avoid awkward leaps, muddy chords and collisions between hands.

Let's look at three different versions of a simple little melody fragment with just a C major chord.

Melody:

All three versions demonstrate our principle of inversion: that a chord retains its basic identity no matter what order its notes appear. A chord with the root note on bottom is said to be in root position; a chord with the third on bottom is said to be in first inversion; a chord with the fifth on bottom is said to be in second inversion. (As we shall see later, bigger chords with more notes have more possible inversions.)

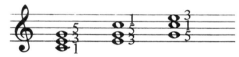

Let's go back to the little melody fragment above. In the first version, we are inverting the C chord in our right hand, while the left hand stays on the root (C) note (doubled an octave higher). Even though our right hand is changing inversions, this is a root position C chord, because the left hand is staying on the root. The right hand is "flip-flopping" in order to accommodate the melody, while putting notes underneath it.

In the second version the right hand is playing only the melody notes while the left hand is alternating the bass note C with an "answering" chord which moves up by inversion. As in the first example, this is still heard as a root position chord because the bass note played on the strong beats (the first and third beats) is still the root of the chord.

In the third version, the actual bass notes of the C chord move up: C-E-G-C. It's still a C major chord, but the changing bass gives these chords different sounds. These inversions are sometimes specifically called for in chord charts. (We will discuss that more a bit later.)

Inversions are used all the time to provide variety to chord voicings, to put chords in more convenient or better sounding registers, and to facilitate moving from chord to chord.

You should now start practicing inverting the four triad types we have presented. A good way to do this is to play a triad with both hands up and down the keyboard. Below is an example for an A minor triad.

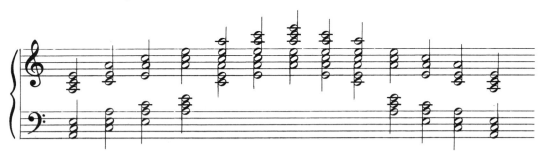

After you get comfortable inverting three-note triads, double the bottom note an octave higher, so that both hands are always spread out into a full position. Using this position helps triads to sound fuller. Below is an example for an Eb major triad.

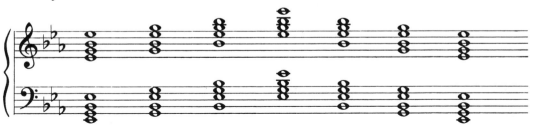

Besides practicing inversions in block chords, try arpeggiating them. Below is an example in G, using full octave positions.

Other variations (of increasing complexity) are helpful in getting the hands to find chord inversions automatically, without having to look down at the keys. Try having your two hands play different inversions of the same chords simultaneously, going up and down the keyboard; this prevents you from getting "locked-in" to a parallel structure between the hands. Below is an example of this for an F augmented chord.

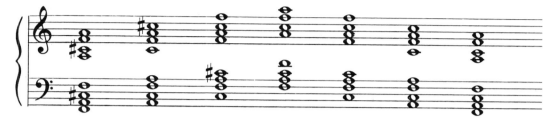

You can also try moving the hands in opposite directions while inverting chords. This might take some concentration at first. Below is an example for an E° chord.

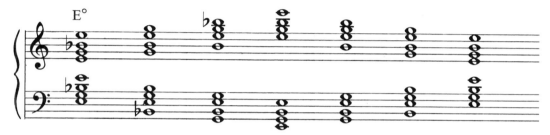

Of course, all these exercises can and should be combined. When practicing any chord, always do it in block form (all notes played together) and in arpeggiated form (one note at a time).

"Spacing" the Chord

9

You may have noticed that the way we have been playing our chords so far, though certainly not bad sounding, is somehow not yet "professional" and seems to lack a certain richness. What do the "pros" do to make their chords sound fuller? Let's play a simple chord progression two different ways and listen to the effects of each.

These are the same chords with the same melody on top. All we did was rearrange the notes of the chords. Let's look at the difference in a bit more detail.

Until now, in discussing the triads, we have only played "closed position" chords. These occur when the three notes of a triad are as close as possible to each other, with no space in between. In a root position triad, this would be the root, with the third directly above it, and the fifth directly above the third. Even when we inverted our accompanying chord, we remained in a closed position, with the chord tones as close as possible to each other.

If you look back at the tune demonstrating the augmented chord, you will see that the very first C major chord is "voiced" with a low C in the bass, a G one octave and a fifth above that, and an E a sixth above the G. Is such a chord, distributed over the distance of 2⅓ octaves, still considered a root position C major triad? *Yes,* because the bass note is still the root of the chord. Such a chord voicing would be considered in "open" position; fake books leave such chord voicing decisions up to the performer. The style and the tempo of the tune, the particular sound quality desired, plus his or her own technical or physical limitations will all affect a player's choice of voicings. Wide open chord voicing, with a large gap filled in between the bass note and the highest note, tends to give us a richer, more orchestral sound. This also allows us to use our two hands in a more balanced fashion, rather than always sticking to a melody-in-the-right-hand-bass-in-the-left-hand formula. The most common way of opening up a chord, and one which provides a warm, resonant sonority, is to have wide spaces between chord tones in the bass and narrow ones towards the treble.

Let's look at some open voicings of all our triads in C root position. Try transposing these voicings (and others of your own creation) into all the keys. Note that we avoid putting the third directly above the root when the bass note is low, otherwise we would produce a muddy sound.

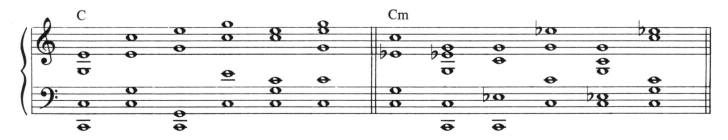

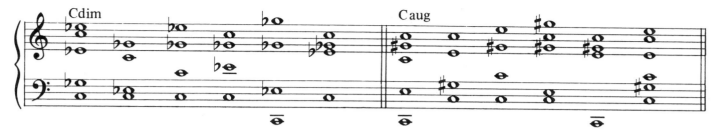

The concept of "spacing out" the chord tones can be applied when the notes are all playing simultaneously, in block fashion, or in succession, i.e., arpeggiated. Let's try a tune using examples of both.

This is a fake chart arrangement of the traditional folk tune "I Gave My Love a Cherry." (Folk tunes like this can usually be harmonized with a variety of chord progressions, since no composer ever wrote down the "right" changes.) Let's look at a realization using simple open chord voicings.

Here we are using a basic two-beat accompaniment — that is, an accompanying chord on each half note. Unlike the previous bass note-chord left hand patterns, here the harmony is distributed between the hands. The effect is more like a choral harmonization; the rhythm is not as strong as it is with the "oom-pah" pattern. We still have the root note played on the downbeat, but here there is a full chord harmonization over it.

There are a few observations about the above example that should be noted. First, when we have a low bass note the interval immediately above it is generally a fifth or an octave. Where we do have a third it is expanded to a tenth (3rd plus octave). Second, the harmonizing note is dictated by the melody. When the melody contains the third of the triad, it is not necessary to add the third to the chord accompaniment underneath; likewise with the fifth. Of course, our root position chords always have the root in the bass, whether it appears in the melody or not. Notice also that in this realization, at times we leave out the fifth of the triad, without creating the feeling that anything is "missing."

This "choral" accompaniment (using open chords) is particularly suitable to a slow, lyrical melody.

Now let's try the same tune using open chords in an arpeggiated, rather than blocked, fashion.

Here we are arpeggiating the triad in the left hand, starting on the root. The melody is up an octave from where it was originally written, in order to make room for the accompaniment, without having to play the bass too low on the keyboard. Playing the melody an octave higher than written is often advisable when playing from a fake book, since they tend to be written out where they fit most easily on the staff, not necessarily where they are played most effectively. (Of course, which octave to play a melody in is determined by the effect the player wishes to achieve, the style of the accompaniment and the need for variety when repeating.)

Notice also that the right hand "helps out" in the arpeggiation. It fills in the harmony note missing from the arpeggio, especially if that note is not contained in the melody. (Since our arpeggio reveals only one chord tone at a time, we need to add at least one other chord tone if our ear is to get a "fix" on the chord quality. For a minor or major triad, the critical chord tone is the third, because it defines the minor or major quality; for a diminished or augmented triad, the critical chord tone is the fifth, because it defines the diminished or augmented quality.)

Although the left hand will generally retain the lion's share of the responsibility for the rhythmic characteristic of the accompaniment, by dividing the harmonic responsibility between the two hands, it is easier to play in a smoothly flowing pattern.

As you might guess, the same principles of "opening up" the chord can be applied to inverted chords. Look at the examples of inverted C major and minor chords in their open positions below.

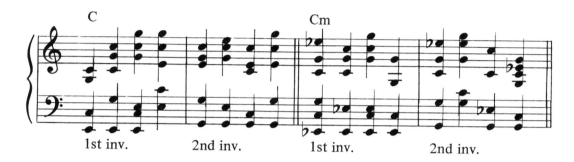

Practice finding these and other voicings for all the triads in all the keys. Get used to finding open hand positions all over the keyboard. This will only come with practice. Try to minimize (and eventually completely avoid) looking at your hands when playing a variety of chord positions.

Inversions (Part 2) – Slash Chords

10

Have you ever looked at the chord symbols in sheet music and seen two different chord letters, separated by a slash mark? It looks as if they are giving you a choice between two chords (or they couldn't make up their minds!).

There is really no mystery here. There are times when a song requires you to play a certain inversion of a chord. Often this is because the composer wants a certain sound, and wishes to tell you so in the chord symbols. How is this done?

The "slash" chord is the simple, practical solution to the problem. The first letter, before the slash, is the chord name. The second letter, after the slash, is the desired bass note. Thus a C major triad in the first inversion (with the third, E, in the bass) would be notated C/E, and an E minor chord in the second inversion would be notated Em/B.

Using this "slash" system, any note, not just a chord tone, could be indicated as the bass note underneath a given chord. For now, however, we will restrict ourselves to talking about their use to notate specific inversions.

Let's look at a melody with two similar accompaniments, one using just root position chords, and the other using slash chords. Below we have a tune harmonized in root position, and following is the same tune using slash chord inversions at selected points. Play both versions and listen to the difference.

In the first version, the very first F major chord is an open voiced root position chord. On the next beat, the left hand plays an "answering" chord. By itself, the second chord would be considered a second inversion F chord (F/C), but in the context of the whole measure, it is considered a continuation of the root position F established on the first beat. In other words, our ear tends to retain the bass note established on a strong beat. If we are using a bass note-chord accompaniment, the bass notes can be connected together as an independent line or melody, while the answering or follow-up chords can be considered part of the preceding bass note (no matter how the answering chords are inverted).

Let's go back to the second version of the melody. It sounds a little more "musical," warmer and perhaps more pleasing to the ear. Let's see why.

Instead of jumping all over the keyboard to hit the root of each chord, the bass line here assumes a smoother, more melodic character. There is more step-wise movement than is possible with root position chords. By giving the bass line a "tune" of its own, there is a more interesting relationship between the bass and the melody. (Try playing only the bass and the melody for each version and you will immediately hear the difference!) This interaction between bass and melody is an important part of good harmony for all kinds of music, be it pop, jazz, rock or classical.

Contemporary popular music tends to be specific in indicating slash chords, while older fake books generally indicate only root chord names. The main reason for this is that the harmonic language of pop music has become a little more sophisticated, and specific inversions and voicings are sometimes needed to get exactly the right sound. Therefore, when looking at a chart for a "Gay 90's" tune, you will usually find very basic chords, whereas when looking at a Billy Joel tune, you can expect something more complicated.

Let us look at an old American folk song harmonized with several inverted triads. (Here we are using the arpeggiated style of accompaniment.)

"Shenandoah"

Realization:

bass line:

By now you should be trying to play your own versions of our fake charts. Remember, your ears must always be the guide in how you are going to accompany a melody. Generally speaking, you will want to be consistent in the accompaniment pattern; don't try to change styles with each measure. Although playing from a fake chart is a kind of improvisation (within a structured harmonic and melodic framework), it might be worthwhile to write out your accompaniment patterns in sketch form at first. It will help you to create and remember good musical ideas, and will give your practicing more structure.

The Major Chord Family

11

You've probably heard a cocktail pianist take a simple melody and make it sound more "sophisticated." Let's see if we can do that ourselves. Here are two versions of the traditional folk song "Kumbaya." Listen carefully to the difference between them.

The second one sounds "jazzier," less like a folk song, doesn't it? Instead of using the triads that we have been working with up to now, we added a fourth note to some of the chords to enrich the sound. The root notes and chord qualities (major or minor) are the same in the two versions, but that fourth note changes our perception of the tune.

A fourth note can be added to all four chord types, but in this chapter we will discuss only the family of chords built on the major triad. There are three additions to the major triad: the sixth, the seventh, and the major seventh.

Major Sixth Chords

The major sixth chord is formed by adding the tone a major sixth above the root (or a whole tone above the fifth) to a major triad. The note added on to a C major triad to make it a sixth chord, then, would be A.

In fake charts, the major sixth chord is usually indicated by the numeral six placed after the chord letter Eb6, for example. Some charts will call it an "added sixth" (abbreviated "add6," as in F#add6). The latter is technically more correct, because, traditionally, chords can only be built using alternating scale tones (i.e., 1-3-5-7, etc.). However, most charts use only the number 6 without creating any confusion.

The major sixth chord, while adding some character to the pure sound of a major triad, is not really dissonant to our ears. In fact, it is so smooth sounding that it can come across as a bit old-fashioned if used extensively. It is frequently acceptable, *within certain musical styles,* to add a sixth to major triads even if the lead sheet (fake chart) doesn't so indicate. A tune like "The Old Gray Mare," for instance, would be written in a fake chart just with triads. Notice how we create a nice effect by adding the major sixth.

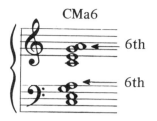

You will recall that the chords formed on the first, fourth and fifth notes of a major scale are all major chords found naturally in the major scale. Each of these chords (the I, IV and V) can also have the major sixth added on without introducing any accidentals (sharps or flats). Most often, this would be done on the I or IV, but not on the V. (This is because the V chord's function in a chord progression is to bring us back to the I chord; our ear tells us it must eventually resolve to the I chord. The addition of the 6th lessens the V's sense of direction, and a strong V-I progression would never occur. This concept will be clarified in the next section.)

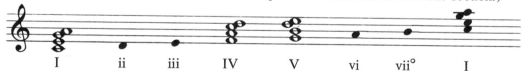

I   ii   iii   IV   V   vi   vii°   I

You can now practice building major sixth chords on all twelve roots.

M 6 chords

37

Major sixth chords, and all of the chords that we will be discussing, may be inverted and played in open positions using the same principles that were applied to triads. The only difference is this: as we add notes to our chords, the number of possible inversions increases. Below, we see how this works for a D6 chord; now there are three possible inversions (built on the 3rd [F#], the 5th [A], and the 6th [B]).

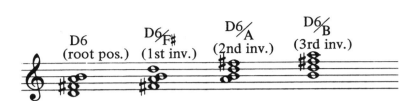

Now, let's look at just a few open voicings of a G6 chord, using root position and first inversion (G6/B) as examples.

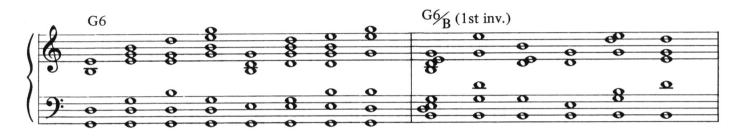

To help you practice inverting the major sixth chords, below is a chart of all the chords with the appropriate bass note for each inversion. Try to create as many different voicings of each chord as you can, so that playing and recognizing them starts to become automatic. Equivalent notes (enharmonics) are put in parentheses.

Chord		1st inv.		2nd inv.		3rd inv.	
C6		/E		/G		/A	
Db6	(C#6)	/F	(E#)	/Ab	(G#)	/Bb	(A#)
D6		/F#		/A		/B	
Eb6	(D#6)	/G	(Fx)	/Bb	(A#)	/C	(B#)
E6		/G#		/B		/C#	
F6		/A		/C		/D	
Gb6	(F#6)	/Bb	(A#)	/Db	(C#)	/Eb	(D#)
G6		/B		/D		/E	
Ab6	(G#6)	/C	(B#)	/Eb	(D#)	/F	(E#)
A6		/C#		/E		/F#	
Bb6	(A#6)	/D	(Cx)	/F	(E#)	/G	(Fx)
B6		/D#		/F#		/G#	

Seventh Chords

Play the chord below:

38

It doesn't seem to want to stay there, does it? It leaves you waiting for the other shoe to drop—it wants to move to a more resolved chord. The resolved chord would be:

The first chord is another member of the four note chord family. It is the seventh chord, sometimes called a *dominant seventh* (to distinguish it from the other types of seventh chords). It is formed by adding the note a minor seventh above the root (a minor third above the fifth) to a major triad. It is indicated by the numeral 7 after the chord letter; A7 or B7, for example. At right is a sample C7 in basic root position.

Seventh chords are built naturally on the V (dominant) chord of the major scale, hence the name dominant seventh. By playing alternating scale tones starting with the fifth note of any major scale (5-7-2-4 of that scale), we will naturally build a dominant seventh chord.

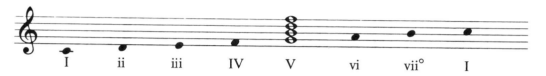

A dominant seventh wants to resolve to the chord lying a fifth below it. In our example at the beginning of this section, our G7 wanted to resolve to a C chord (major in this case, but it can resolve just as well to minor). Because dominant chords have this special impetus, their most traditional use is to bring the music back home to its tonic key (V7- I). If one creates a dominant seventh on notes other than the V, this will push the music temporarily to new keys. This is the reason that a V6 chord will not occur as often as a V7; the latter is more functional because it helps pull the music back to its home tonic key.

There is a special use of seventh chords that is completely outside the function described above, and that is in blues and blues-derived music. In blues (which in its simpler forms is built solely on I, IV and V chords), all chords are dominant chords, yet there is no need to resolve them. A blues pattern in C consists of C7, F7 and G7 chords. This requires changing some notes in the normal C major scale, yet there is no confusion about which key we are in. This is because the sound of the dominant seventh has become the "norm" in this music.

You should now try to form dominant sevenths on all the roots.

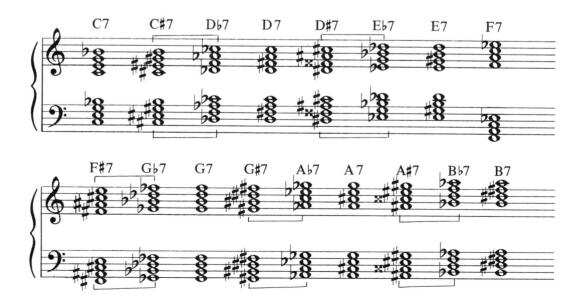

Like all four-note chords, there are three possible inversions of seventh chords. Slash chord inversions are not uncommon with seventh chords, especially in some contemporary popular songs.

Following are few voicings of a C7 chord in root position and inverted positions. Notice that in the slash chord indication of the third inversion, we call the chord a C/B♭ rather than a C7/B♭, because the seventh is the bass note itself. This is common practice. In fact, these chords are often voiced just as implied by the slash mark; the triad is played in the right hand, while the bass note is played in the left hand (as seen in the last example below).

When inversions are notated by slash marks, it is usually intended that the bass note be clearly heard. That is why it is often played separated from the rest of the chord.

Below is a list of all the seventh chord inversions.

Chord		1st inv.		2nd inv.		3rd inv.	
C7		/E		/G		/B♭	
D♭7	(C#7)	/F	(E#)	/A♭	(G#)	/C♭	(B)
D7		/F#		/A		/C	
E♭7	(D#7)	/G	(F𝄪)	/B♭	(A#)	/D♭	(C#)
E7		/G#		/B		/D	
F7		/A		/C		/E♭	
G♭7	(F#7)	/B♭	(A#)	/D♭	(C#)	/F♭	(E)
G7		/B		/D		/F	
A♭7	(G#)	/C	(B#)	/E♭	(D#)	/G♭	(F#)
A7		/C#		/E		/G	
B♭7	(A#7)	/D	(C𝄪)	/F	(E#)	/A♭	(G#)
B7		/D#		/F#		/A	

Major Seventh Chords

You will recall our jazzed-up version of "Kumbaya" at the beginning of this chapter. The chord that was primarily responsible for that more sophisticated sound was another member of the major family, the major seventh chord. It only takes one major seventh chord at the beginning of a tune to give it that contemporary color.

V7   IMa7

The major seventh is formed by adding a note a major seventh above the root (a major third above the fifth) to a major triad. There are several symbols for these chords used in chord charts; "maj7," "ma7" or "M7" (with a capital M to distinguish it from minor) are most common. Some charts (especially jazz oriented ones) use a small triangle, with or without a 7, such as A △ or A△7. Here is a C major 7.

The major seventh chord is very common in today's pop music. You won't see it much in folk and country music, older popular music or traditional folk songs. It has a slight dissonance to it that adds a pleasant spiciness to the harmonic sound. Unlike the dominant seventh (which needs to resolve to another chord), the major seventh can be satisfying as a final chord. (In fact, ending a song on a major seventh arpeggio is a typical cocktail pianist's device.)

ped.

Like the major sixth, it is appropriate in some styles of music to play a major seventh instead of a simple triad, even if the chart doesn't indicate this. The use of a major seventh would be most common on the I and IV chords of a major key, where they can be formed diatonically.

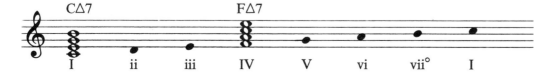

I   ii   iii   IV   V   vi   vii°   I

You can now form major sevenths on all twelve roots.

Obviously, there are three possible inversions of the major seventh chord. Slash chord inversions are fairly common, especially in the third inversion (C/B, for example). They usually occur when the bass line begins a descending major scale from the root, while a static major triad is retained over it. (There'll be more on this type of chord formation later, when we get into voice leading.)

Let's look at a few possible voicings of the major seventh chord in C (for all the inversions).

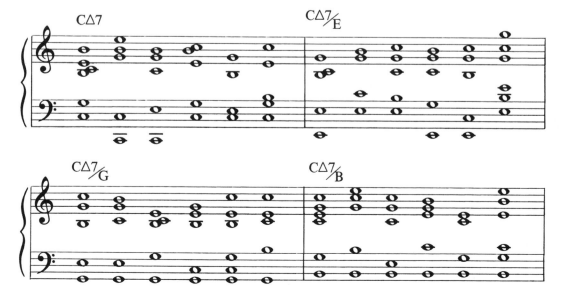

42

Below are all the major seventh chords with their inverted bass tones.

Chord		1st inv.		2nd inv.		3rd inv.	
C M7		/E		/G		/B	
Db M7	(C# M7)	/F	(E#)	/Ab	(G#)	/C	(B#)
D M7		/F#		/A		/C#	
Eb M7	(D# M7)	/G	(F𝄪)	/Bb	(A#)	/D	(C𝄪)
E M7		/G#		/B		/D#	
F M7		/A		/C		/E	
Gb M7	(F# M7)	/Bb	(A#)	/Db	(C#)	/F	(E#)
G M7		/B		/D		/F#	
Ab M7	(G# M7)	/C	(B#)	/Eb	(D#)	/G	(F𝄪)
A M7		/C#		/E		/G#	
Bb M7	(A# M7)	/D	(C𝄪)	/F	(E#)	/A	(G𝄪)
B M7		/D#		/F#		/A#	

This completes our major chord family. Let's begin to apply these chords to some musical examples.

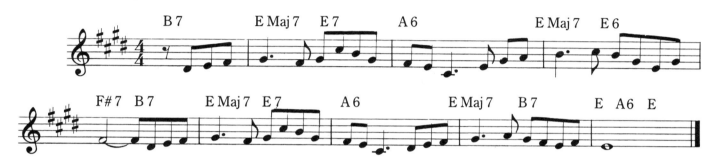

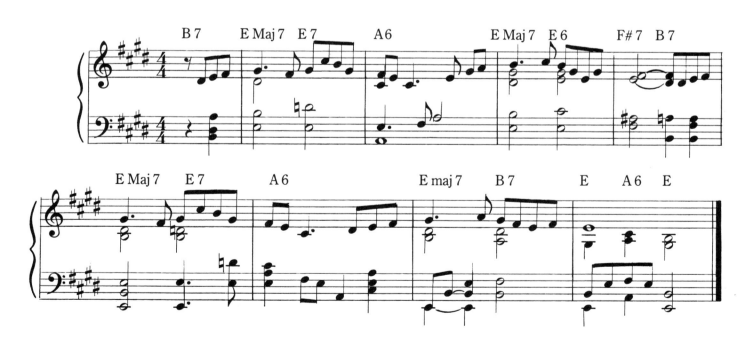

Our first example is the beginning of the familiar tune "Londonderry Air." Our arrangement blocks out the chords using very little arpeggiation, in root positions. Notice how we use the chord tone provided by the melody to help frame out the chord, as in the first measure where the melodically repeated G#s provide the third of our E maj7 and E7 chords.

Notice that with seventh and major seventh chords (and most big chords in general), we can often leave out the fifth without any great harm; the ear can still "understand" the chord. (The situation is more ambiguous for a major sixth, because if you leave out the fifth, it becomes a first inversion minor chord. This is not necessarily bad, but it does make the chord less identifiable as a major sixth.)

Pay attention to the way you voice chords in the blocked out style. Generally speaking, when the bass note is low, it's better to avoid closed position chords in the left hand. We might use the fifth, the sixth, the seventh or the octave as the next highest tone over the bass note, but rarely the third, which is used only if the chord is positioned high enough to avoid a muddy sound.

The second musical example is in an early jazz "stride piano" style.

Note: Bracketed notes in l.h. are optional. Add notes under r.h. melody as before.

Here we use inversions of the major family chords. These inversions allow for a pleasant ascending bass line (F-F#-G-G#-A). The accompaniment is the bass note-chord pattern that is the essence of the stride style. The faster one plays a stride-type pattern like this, the more difficult (and unnecessary) it is to grab all four notes in the left hand after striking the bass note. A strong bass line like this one practically carries the harmony by itself.

Try this same tune in a different arrangement, using blocked out chords (no isolated bass note) in the left hand. Below is an example of the first three measures of the left hand done in this way.

44

Notice that this puts an accent on every beat instead of on every other beat. Without the isolated bass note on the first and third beats of the measure, we tend to hear four beats per measure. (This is called "playing in four," as opposed to "playing in two.") In this block chord style, the full chord must be played in the inversion dictated by the slash chord symbol; there is no separate bass note to "set up" the correct inversion as there was in the stride-style realization.

The third example using major family chords is a modern pop-style ballad.

This tune uses major seventh chords heavily for the I and IV chords, a common occurrence in this type of song. We have arpeggiated the accompaniment in an open chord in the left hand, which gives us a pleasantly "rolling" pattern. The right hand supplies the "fourth note" of the chord, either in the melody itself or in the harmony beneath it. This type of accompaniment works well for slow ballads. Good use of the sustain pedal is also important to connect the chord tones so the full chord is allowed to sound. (Since heavy pedalling can make block chords out of arpeggios, be careful not to space the chords too closely above a low bass note.)

Our fourth musical example is the "Gay 90's" standard, "While Strolling Through the Park One Day."

Here again we use our alternating bass note and chord pattern, but notice that, in addition to alternating the root and the fifth in the bass (measures 2 and 4), we also alternate root and third (measures 1 and 3). This pattern works especially well on a dominant seventh chord that resolves to its tonic (V7-I), because the 3rd of the dominant chord just ascends a semi-tone to the root of the next chord (E-F, F#-G). Of course, to use this movement, the chord must last long enough; in measure 6, where there are two chords, we only have time for a single bass note for each chord. Notice also that we have used a major sixth chord a few times where only a major triad was indicated in the fake chart. Be aware that a fake chart is a general guideline only, and the more experience and skill you develop, the more you can add your own ideas.

The Minor Chord Family

12

Just as a fourth note can be added to a major triad, so can one be added to a minor triad. In fact, the same three intervals that are added to the major triad are added to the minor. The only difference between the three chords we are going to learn now and those we just finished discussing is that the third in each of the new chords is minor.

Minor Sixth Chords

Anyone who has ever been to a wedding ceremony has heard a minor sixth chord as the very first chord of one of the world's most recognizable pieces of music.

Try the same melody using a plain A minor triad instead of the A minor sixth as written (leave out the F#). By comparison, it really sounds lacking in character, doesn't it?

The minor sixth chord is built by adding the note a major sixth above the root (a whole step above the fifth) to a minor triad. In chord charts, it is labeled min6, m6 or occasionally -6. To the right is a C min6.

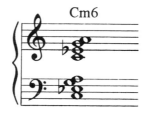

The most common use of the minor sixth is as part of a iv min6 - V7 - i progression in a minor key. The "Wedding March" was one example of this; below is another.

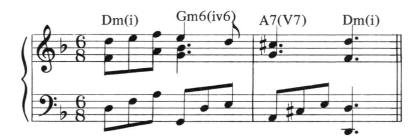

Sometimes, the tonic chord in a minor key is played as a minor sixth. This is done in Latin dance tunes and in some big band tunes, such as "Caravan." In general, though, it is not played too often (except as a "passing chord"), because of its somewhat dissonant sound. It is not nearly as pleasant sounding as its counterpart, the major sixth chord, because in the minor sixth chord, the interval between the third and the sixth of the chord is the highly unresolved *tritone* (three whole tones).

You may invert minor sixths using the same principles we applied to the rest of the chords. When they are put in the third inversion, they become identical to another chord we will be looking at later, the half-diminished chord. For this reason, these two chords are sometimes used interchangeably in different song books, according to the whims of their editors. (For the same reason, you will probably never see a slash chord notation of a minor sixth chord in third inversion.)

Below are a few typical open voicings of a D min6 in root position as well as first and second inversion.

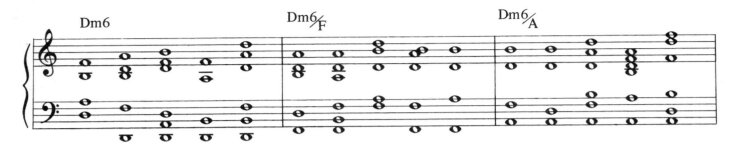

As we have done for the other chords, below is a list of all the minor sixth chords in inversions.

Chord	1st inv.		2nd inv.		3rd inv.	
Cm6	/Eb		/G		/A	
Dbm6 (C#m6)	/Fb	(E)	/Ab	(G#)	/Bb	(A#)
Dm6	/F		/A		/B	
Ebm6 (D#m6)	/Gb	(F#)	/Bb	(A#)	/C	(B#)
Em6	/G		/B		/C#	
Fm6	/Ab		/C		/D	
Gbm6 (F#m6)	/Bb	(A)	/Db	(C#)	/Eb	(D#)
Gm6	/Bb		/D		/E	
Abm6 (G#m6)	/Cb	(B)	/Eb	(D#)	/F	(E#)
Am6	C		/E		/F#	
Bbm6 (A#m6)	/Db	(C#)	/F	(E#)	/G	(Fx)
Bm6	/D		/F#		/G#	

Now, here are minor sixth chords built on all twelve tones.

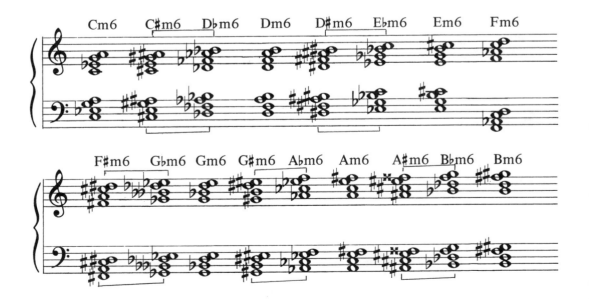

Minor Seventh Chords

The most common minor chord is the minor seventh. You will find it in tunes from show music to jazz to rock and roll. It is very frequently used as part of a ii min7 - V7 -I(maj7) progression, which can be found in countless popular songs, such as "Autumn Leaves" and "I've Got You Under My Skin." Here is an example of this chord:

The minor seventh chord is formed by adding the note a minor seventh above the root (minor third above the fifth) to a minor triad. The seventh is tacked onto a minor triad as a matter of course in almost all jazz arrangements, and also in a great deal of popular music. It is notated as min7, m7 or -7. At right is a C min7 in closed root position.

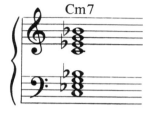

When a minor seventh is put into first inversion (with the third of the chord on the bottom), it turns into a major sixth chord rooted on the bottom note. For instance, an A min7/C (1st inversion of an A min7) looks just like a C6, and a C6/A looks like an Am7 in root position.

Does this mean that these chords are interchangeable? Not necessarily, because even if two different chords actually consist of the same notes, the particular way we voice them can influence what we perceive to be the root note, thus affecting their harmonic purpose. We would be less likely to duplicate the note A in a C6 than in A min7. The harmonic context—that is, the chords that precede and follow —will usually help determine the proper labeling in these cases of "identical twin" chords.

Here are a few two-handed voicings of an Em7 in root and inverted positions.

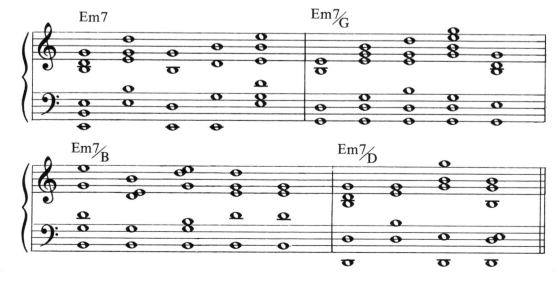

A slash chord third inversion of a minor seventh (E min/D) most often occurs when the bass begins a descending scale down from the root of the chord, while the minor chord above it remains stationary.

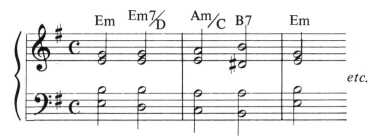

Below are all the minor sevenths and their enharmonic equivalents with inversions.

Chord	1st inv.		2nd inv.		3rd inv.	
Cm7	/Eb		/G		/Bb	
Dbm7 (C#m7)	/Fb	(E)	/Ab	(G#)	/Cb	(B)
Dm7	/F		/A		/C	
Ebm7 (D#m7)	/Gb	(F#)	/Bb	(A#)	/Db	(C#)
Em7	/G		/B		/D	
Fm7	/Ab		/C		/Eb	
Gbm7 (F#m7)	/Bbb	(A)	/Db	(C#)	/Fb	(E)
Gm7	/Bb		/D		/F	
Abm7 (G#m7)	/Cb	(B)	/Eb	D#)	/Gb	(F#)
Am7	/C		/E		/G	
Bbm7 (A#m7)	/Db	(C#)	/F	(E#)	/Ab	(G#)
Bm7	/D		/F#		/A	

Here are the minor sevenths in root position. Practice them as they appear, and in inversion.

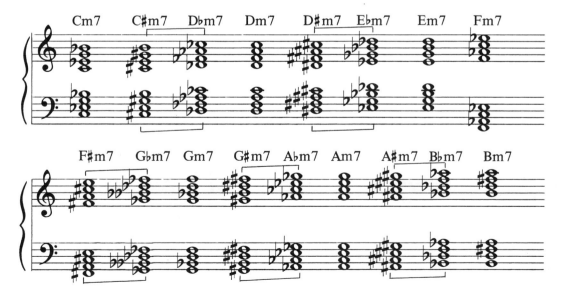

Minor +7 Chords

This is a fairly "modern" chord that you won't find in old-fashioned sing-along tunes, traditional folk music and other simpler harmonic styles. You will find its rather strong, somewhat dissonant sound most often in jazz. It will often be seen as a "passing" chord in a series of minor chords with one moving voice.

This chord is formed by adding the note a major seventh above the root (a major third above the fifth) to a minor triad. Below is a Cm+7.

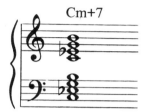 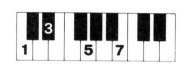

Because this chord is a little more unusual than the others we have seen, its labeling is less standardized. It is notated by min(maj7), -(△7), min#7, min ♮7 (used when the regular 7th would be a flat), or some other variation of these.

As a spicy expansion of a minor triad, the m+7 chord is sometimes used by jazz musicians to add color to a plainer chord. When specifically notated on a chord chart, one of its most common uses is in this familiar sounding pattern:

Notice here that the basic A minor chord stays put while the lowest note in the right hand moves down chromatically. A common variation of this pattern is to have this movement occur in the bass voice.

Below are a few sample voicings of an A min+7 in root and inverted positions.

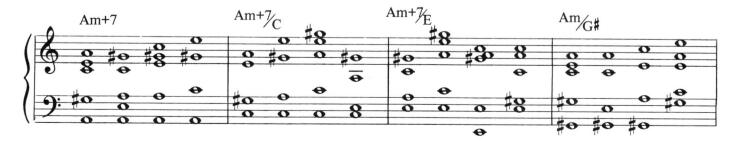

Here are all the min+7 chords in root position.

Below are the same chords with bass notes for each inversion.

Chord	1st inv.		2nd inv.		3rd inv.	
Cm+7	/Eb		/G		/B	
Db(C#)m+7	/Fb	(E)	/Ab	(G#)	/C	(B#)
Dm+7	/F		/A		/C#	
Eb(D#)m+7	/Gb	(F#)	/Bb	(A#)	/D	(C𝄪)
Em+7	/G		/B		/D#	
Fm+7	/Ab		/C		/E	
Gb(F#)m+7	/Bbb	(A)	/Db	(C#)	/F	(E#)
Gm+7	/Bb		/D		/F#	
Ab(G#)m+7	/Cb	(B)	/Eb	(D#)	/G	(F𝄪)
Am+7	/C		/E		/G#	
Bb(A#)m+7	/Db	(C#)	/F	(E#)	/A	(G𝄪)
Bm+7	/D		/F#		/A#	

Now let's try to use all these minor family chords in some tunes. Our first example (in Em) is in a typical contemporary romantic ballad style. (It probably sounds a lot like some movie themes you've heard!)

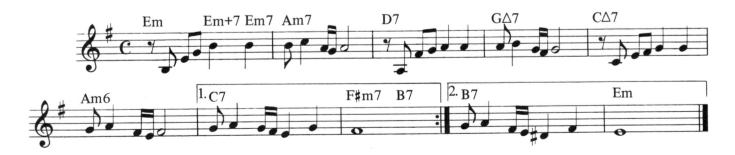

Here in our suggested realization, we move the melody up an octave from where it is written in the fake chart. Why? One reason is that this type of tune sounds good with the melody "tinkling" in a higher range. (Remember, fake books always put the melody in a comfortable written range; there will be times when you want to play it in a higher octave.) Another reason is that the accompaniment pattern used here would collide with the melody, were it played in its written range.

The accompaniment pattern suggested here is a simple one. The bass note provides the root of the chord on the downbeat, which is followed by various inversions for the rest of the measure. An additional chord tone is occasionally added under the melody in the right hand. (An unadorned melody suspended high above chord changes can sound wonderfully lyrical.)

Notice in the first measure that the Em - Em+7 - Em7 is accomplished by the movement of one voice in the left hand. It is important to know that every time you see a new chord written *you don't have to play all the notes of that chord* if some of the chord tones were stated in the preceding chord or chords. Another thing to take note of in the accompaniment is the way it "fills in" at the points where the melody comes to rest, providing rhythmic continuity throughout. This can be seen in measure 8, when the melody note is held, and the left hand arpeggiates the chords in eighth notes. Notice that the two sustained notes (melody and harmony) in the right hand are chord tones for both chords in the accompaniment.

Now, let's look at another tune with a different accompaniment style.

*note inversion of chord
for variety.*

Continue on your own using
similar patterns.

This is a Bossa Nova-style tune. The accompaniment here not only has to play the chords, but must do so in the characteristic Bossa rhythm. (We will deal more with specific rhythmic accompaniments later.) Notice how the rhythmic figure appears constantly, sometimes in the left hand, and sometimes in the right hand. When the melody is active, it is easier to keep a counter rhythm in the accompaniment (e.g., m.1-2, 9-10). When the melody is static, the right hand becomes free to play this figure, so the left hand can be more active (e.g., m.3-4, 11-12). Observe that we keep the chords voiced in the mid-range of the keyboard. These sixth and seventh chords in close spacing will sound muddy if we play them too low on the keyboard. Even the closed position Gm7 in the second measure might get too thick and heavy if we pedal the whole chord instead of detaching the bass note from the rest of the chord.

In measures 6-7, we have a Gm7-C7-F△7 progression. This is an example of our previously mentioned IIm7-V7-I progression. Notice how the notes of the chords in our realization move in stepwise motion from chord tone to chord tone.

This smooth movement of melody and harmony lines is part of the issue of voice leading, which will be more fully explored later. Good voice leading comes with experience and practice, and it is one of the essential characteristics of a basic professional style of playing.

Diminished Sevenths, Half-Diminished Sevenths and Altered Fifth Chords

13

N ow that we have discussed the addition of sevenths to our major and minor triads, we can complete all the types of seventh chords by adding sevenths to the other triads.

Diminished Seventh Chords

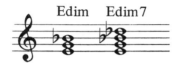

The diminished seventh is not too different in sound than the diminished triad.

You can hear that it doesn't change the character much. As you see, this chord is formed by adding a diminished seventh interval (a minor seventh becomes diminished when it is lowered a half step) above the root note of a diminished triad. The chord consists of three consecutive minor thirds. Below is a C diminished seventh. Diminished sevenths may be labeled by the signs "dim7" or "°7."

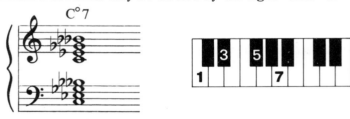

Because diminished sevenths are built on equal intervals and divide up the octave equally, the distances between the notes remain the same when the chord is inverted. Let us look at a D dim7 chord in its three possible inversions.

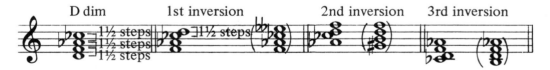

Since each inversion of a diminished seventh chord can be considered a root position diminished chord on its own, we find that *there are actually only three diminished seventh chords.* For this reason, lead sheets don't need to indicate these chords in inversion. Instead of notating "Fdim7/Ab," it is much simpler to write "Abdim7." Below are the three diminished seventh chords, in root position and inverted position, grouped together.

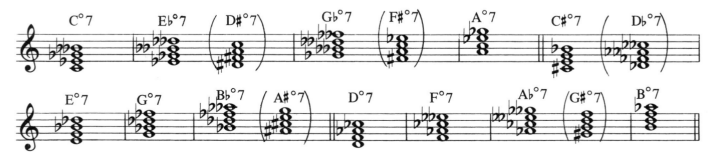

Fake books tend to be indifferent about distinguishing between sevenths and plain diminished triads, since the two forms have pretty much the same effect. Therefore, most of the time, you can assume it's okay to play a diminished seventh, even if the chart indicates only a diminished triad.

Here are a few open voicings of diminished seventh chords.

Half Diminished Seventh Chords

The half diminished chord often seems to mystify musicians. Many players who are quite comfortable with all the chords we've mentioned so far react with a blank look when asked to play a half diminished chord. Relax. Playing this chord does not require a lifetime of meditation and study. In fact, it's only an inversion of a chord we've already studied: the minor sixth chord. At right is a Cm6 chord. If we "flip it over" to its third inversion — lo and behold! — we have created an A half diminished chord.

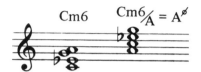

This chord is called half diminished because it is constructed by adding the note a minor seventh above the root to a diminished triad. Thus it differs from a regular (or "full") diminished seventh, which consists of a series of stacked minor thirds. At right is a C half diminished.

The normal symbols for the half diminished chord is a slash mark through the circle symbol of the diminished chord, as in Aø. It is also sometimes labelled a min7♭5. The logic for this is understandable. If you take a minor seventh chord and then lower its fifth a semi-tone, you end up with a half diminished. At right is a demonstration.

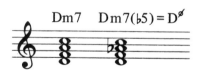

Here are all the half diminished chords in root position.

Because of its equivalence to an inverted minor sixth chord, it would be unlikely to see a half diminished chord notated in inversion as a slash chord. Below are a few open voicings of a C°.

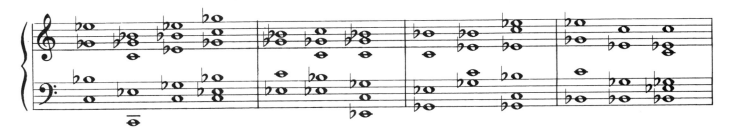

+5 Chords

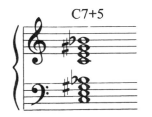

We've already looked at augmented chords as triads. Chords bigger than triads can have the fifth of the chord augmented, or sharped. The most common case of this would be an alteration of a dominant seventh chord. Such a chord would be notated as "7 aug5," "aug7," "7(+5)," "7(#5)," "+7" or "7+."

This chord usually functions as a regular dominant seventh chord, but the augmented fifth gives it added flavor. Listen to the difference in sound in the following passage using a regular dominant seventh chord in the second measure, and an augmented seventh in the fourth measure. (Notice how the only change is the use of G# in the left hand instead of G.) Of course, such an alteration of the fifth requires a melody that "fits" the chord.

Here are all the 7 (+5) chords.

A major seventh chord can also have the fifth augmented. This is not as common, but it might be seen in some contemporary jazz charts. Below is an example of such a chord in E♭.

A minor chord with an augmented fifth becomes an inversion of a major chord built on that augmented fifth, so such a notation would be unusual. You might see it on rare occasions as a means of drawing attention to the movement of one voice within a stationary minor chord.

-5 Chords

Just as a dominant seventh chord can have its fifth augmented, so can it have its fifth diminished (flatted). Again, this is a more colorful variation of a plain dominant seventh, and it is generally used for similar functions. This is a good chord to know, as it is very common in jazz and contemporary Latin tunes (such as the Bossa Nova), and it is frequently used by jazz players as a substitute for a plain dominant seventh, melody line permitting. Listen to the difference between the first and second measures of the following passage.

Below is a flatted fifth on a C7 chord. A flatted fifth may be notated as "-5" or "♭5."

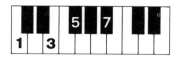

Let's look at some examples using the chords discussed in this chapter. Our first example is a simple waltz melody with some pleasant harmonic twists provided by these altered chords.

Notice that the left hand plays the chords in a simple closed position until the end of the melodic phrase (measure 4), where the Bb7+5 chord is divided between the hands. In measures 7-8, where the C7 becomes a C7+5, the only note that changes is the G. If you don't hold the C in the bass through these two measures, the ear will still hear it in the second measure. Using a bass note to "set up" a chord (even though the note is not repeated) is an important technique that helps make our playing a lot more flexible.

To illustrate this principle further, look at measure 12. The F# diminished chord will be heard as having a C in the bass. Inversions usually don't matter with diminished sevenths. In this particular example, the retention of the C in the bass works well because it makes for smooth voice leading.

Our next example is a ballad. Our accompaniment alternates from an eighth note arpeggio pattern to blocked out chords, depending on the melodic rhythm. When the melody is held, the accompaniment is in eighth notes; when the melody moves in eighth notes the accompaniment is in quarter notes. Besides providing variety to the accompaniment, this allows one to concentrate on one hand at a time. An advanced player may be able to improvise an accompaniment which requires tremendous rhythmic independence of the hands, but for most players, allowing one hand to rest while the other is more active is usually an advisable way to play a tune. (This is why sheet music sometimes seems awkward to play; the arranger tries to include several instrumental and vocal parts from a recording in a piano reduction, making for complicated rhythms.)

Realization:

Suspended Chords

14

A suspension is something left hanging. Musical suspensions are left hanging, too. Listen to the example below, which you may recognize as a typical ending for works of a dramatic or religious nature.

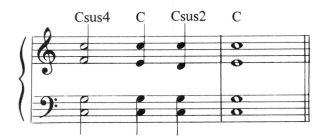

In classical theory, a suspension is a non-chord tone (a note not found in the triad) a step above a chord tone, held over from the previous chord, resolving to a chord tone. In today's pop music, suspended chords no longer need to be set up or resolved, although they frequently are.

The most common suspended chord is the suspended fourth. In this type of chord (be it a triad or a four [or more] note chord), the note that is the third of the chord is raised a semi-tone to the fourth. Below are examples for a C major triad and a C7 chord. Suspensions are usually indicated by the abbreviation "sus."

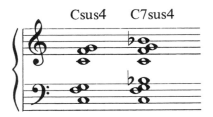

If the symbol "sus" is used without any number, assume that a suspended fourth is desired. There is also a "sus 2." In this chord, a major second above the root is substituted for the third of the chord.

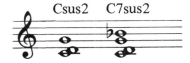

Some fake books will simply write a 2 or 4 after the chord letter to indicate a suspension, e.g., C2 or C4. This is not a terribly good practice, but it does occasionally occur.

Let's try a tune using some suspended chords.

This example is a cha-cha type Latin tune. Our realization has a syncopated left hand, but the pattern is simple: closed position chords with just the suspended note moving. After the repeat, we vary the rhythmic pattern slightly and open the chord position. Notice here (i.e., measure 12) that when the suspended chord resolves, the root note isn't repeated in the bass until the last beat; we still hear it from the suspended chord. Notice also the little bass fill in the second ending (in parentheses). This is to continue the rhythm when the melody comes to rest. It is more effective than banging out an F triad for two measures. The D note in this fill is not really a chord tone (unless you want to consider this an F6 chord), but is there to allow for some melodic movement.

We have now learned our basic chords. All the chords we will discuss in the next two chapters are just expansions of these. Ninths, elevenths and thirteenths may sound complicated, but once you understand the basic principles of chord construction, you won't have much trouble with them.

Ninth Chords

15

Just as we add a seventh above the root of a triad to make a seventh chord, we can add a chord tone a ninth above the root to make a ninth chord. The interval of the ninth (as are all intervals over an octave) is a *compound interval.* It is composed of a smaller interval, a second, plus an octave.

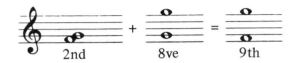

You might be asking yourself what the difference is between a ninth chord and a suspended second chord, since both seem to add the same note under a different name. There are several differences. First, a ninth chord will usually contain the third of the chord. Second, a ninth chord is assumed to include the seventh as well, while a "sus2" would have to notate the seventh if desired ("sus2 add7").

Dominant Ninths

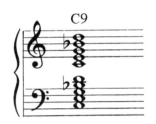

When just the numeral 9 is written after the chord letter, this means a dominant ninth (just as a plain 7 means a dominant seventh). This is constructed by adding a note a major ninth above the root to a seventh chord. At left is a full root position C9 chord.

This chord is usually used to "fatten up" a dominant seventh chord. Sometimes it is indicated in a fake chart simply because the melody adds the ninth. Here is an example of this.

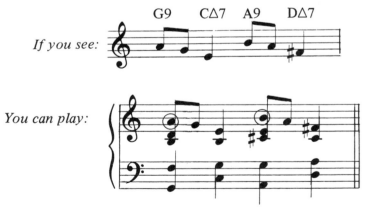

With ninth chords, we can sometimes leave out the fifth. Below are some examples of ninth chord voicings in A.

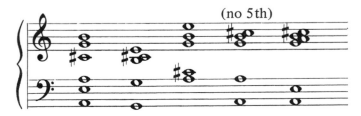

64

Just as we altered the fifth of seventh chords, so can we alter the fifth of ninth chords. These alterations would be indicated by such symbols as "9(b5)" or "9(-5)", and "9(#5)" or "9(+5)" or "aug9."

These chords are just more alterations of regular dominant ninth chords, and are similarly used. Here are all the dominant ninth chords.

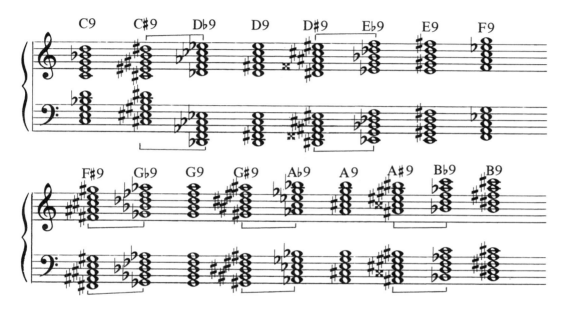

Minor Ninths

The only difference between a minor ninth chord and the dominant ninth chord just discussed is that the minor ninth is built on a minor triad; the added note is still a major ninth above the root of the chord. At right is a C minor ninth in closed root position.

Just as the dominant ninth chord adds "flavor" to the dominant seventh, so does the addition of a ninth to a minor seventh chord change its color. A ii min7 - V7 - I chord change can be enriched by substituting ii min9 - V9 - I maj7, for example.

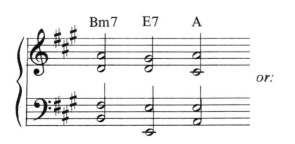

or:

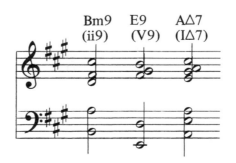

Here are a few examples of minor ninth chord voicings built from the root E.

Below are all the minor ninth chords to practice.

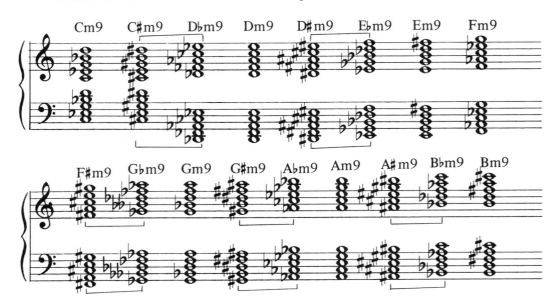

Major Ninths

This chord has the same major ninth above the root added to a major seventh chord. It is used much the way a regular major seventh is; you will find it mostly in the more sophisticated ballads and standards. It would be notated by the symbol "maj9," "△9" or occasionally "M9."

As with all these larger chords (where there is no altered fifth), the fifth of the chord can be omitted. Let's look at a few sample voicings for an F major ninth chord.

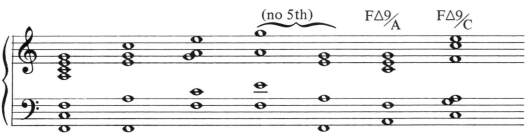

Here are all the major ninths in root position.

You will notice that the top three notes of the major ninth chord form a major triad built on the fifth of another major triad. For instance, the top three notes of the C maj 9 chord (in closed root position) compose a G major triad, the dominant of C. If we leave out the third of the chord (the note E), we will have a G chord over a C bass, or by slash notation G/C. This is one specific voicing of a major ninth chord that has become popular recently with many songwriters. Some chord charts will say "maj9 (no 3rd)" (or similar notation), while others will indicate the chord by slash designation (whatever the particular chord letters are).

Other Ninth Chords

In all three aforementioned ninth chords (major, minor and dominant), the interval between the root and the ninth of the chord (in closed root position) is a major ninth. In a dominant ninth, the ninth itself is occasionally sharped or flatted (the flatted ninth is more common). These would be written as a "7♭9" or a "7#9." Below are these chromatically altered dominant ninth chords in C.

Notice that the top three notes of the root position $b5b9$ form a major triad built a diminished fifth above the root. This can be helpful in getting the fingers to find this chord.

Here is a typical jazz application of the $b5b9$ chord in G minor.

The #9 chord is not seen as often as the $b9$. The interval of the sharped (or augmented) ninth is equivalent to a minor tenth (octave + min 3) above the root. So, this chord contains both the major third and what appears to be the minor third. If not voiced properly, this chord can sound ugly and ambiguous. To avoid this, voice the #9 note *above* the third and play the 7th in between (that helps the ear "understand" it as a 9th rather than a 3rd).

The #9 chord is actually heard a lot more than would at first appear, because in the "blues scale" a minor third in the melody is played against a dominant seventh in the harmony.

Because of the equivalence of the minor third and augmented ninth intervals, the #9 chord has been given some odd names in chord charts, including "major/minor," or "7 (add min 3)."

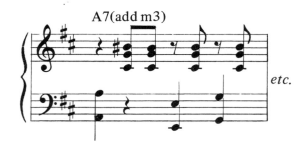

Two other ninth chords will occasionally appear. One is the suspended ninth (or the ninth chord with no seventh). The other is the 6/9, which indicates a major triad with both a major sixth and a major ninth added (but no seventh). This is an airy sounding chord, particularly when voiced with two superimposed perfect fourth intervals.

Eleventh and Thirteenth Chords

Chords can continue to be expanded past the ninth to elevenths and thirteenths. Let's look at them so that you won't be mystified by their occasional appearance.

Elevenths

A plain "11" would indicate a dominant ninth chord with the note an eleventh above the root (octave plus a perfect fourth) added on. At right are two examples, one with a ninth and one with a flatted ninth.

These are obviously a lot of notes (more than one can play with one hand), and the chord can sound very muddy when played in closed spacing. Such a chord is more easily handled (both in terms of finding it on the keyboard and voicing it in a way that doesn't sound too thick) if it is renamed. We could take the top three or four notes as a chord, and indicate the root using slash chord notation. While you will not see a C11 or a C11b9 too often, you will frequently see a Bb/C or a Gm7/C or a Bbm/C or a Bbm6/C. These "modern" voicings of eleventh chords (without a third and sometimes with no fifth) have become very common in the contemporary pop vocabulary. Below are some typical examples.

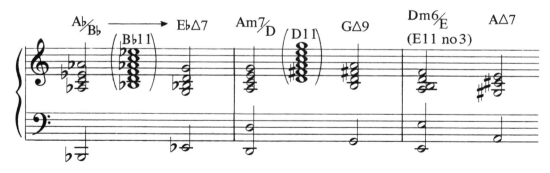

There is one eleventh chord that is more likely to be called an eleventh (rather than a slash chord). It is the sharp 11. Here, the added note lies an augmented 11th (octave plus augmented fourth) above the root. The #11 is usually added onto a dominant chord, but, once in a while, it also shows up in major seventh chords.

Thirteenth Chords

Technically, a thirteenth chord is an eleventh chord with the note a thirteenth above the root added (octave plus major sixth). But it is most often played as a dominant seventh chord with the thirteenth added, as seen in the example here. (A major 13 chord would use the major seventh, rather than the dominant seventh.)

This chord differs from the sixth chord in that the seventh of the chord is included.

Voice Leading

17

There was a time when composers and musicians didn't think about chords (and in fact this is true of many modern composers). Chords and harmony were a by-product or combination of all the individual melodies or "voices." The manner in which those voices move is known as *voice leading*.

One of the reasons we need good voice leading is that it makes our chord changes more fluid. The giveaway of an amateur is that his playing jumps all over the keyboard when going from one chord to another. If a player is not experienced in finding chord inversions, the natural tendency is to play all the chords in root position. By using inversions, we can vary the distance and direction of the individual voices. In addition, tones that are shared by two successive chords (common tones) can be sustained or repeated in the same voice, so that there is a "connecting link" between the chords. Below is a simple four voice progression in C (I-IV-I-V-I) with poor voice leading (parallel movement), and with good "classical" voice leading.

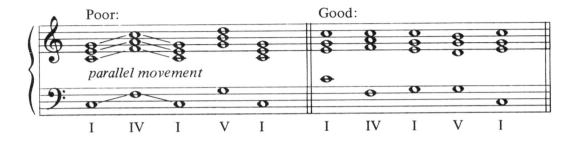

Notice that in the good example none of the voices, except the bass, move more than a step at a time.

How does this apply to playing music from fake books? One should try to change chords with an economy of motion. Make yourself aware of the common tones of frequently used chord progressions, so that your fingers don't shift awkwardly when "making the changes." If you find yourself continually lifting your hands off the keyboard, your voice leading could be better.

How does one "read" the voice leading implied by the chord symbols? This is one area in which fake charts (which usually attempt to simplify music) can .nake things difficult (or at least difficult looking). Perhaps you've seen chord charts where three, four or even more complicated looking chords are crowded into one measure, and you've wondered how it's possible to make those changes so quickly. More often than not, these measures contain only one main chord, and all the other symbols are there to point out the movement of a voice in that chord (it may be the bass or an inner voice).

Let's look more closely at voice leading in the bass. The use of inversions allows for a smooth bass line. Here is an example.

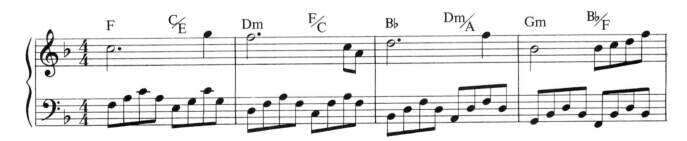

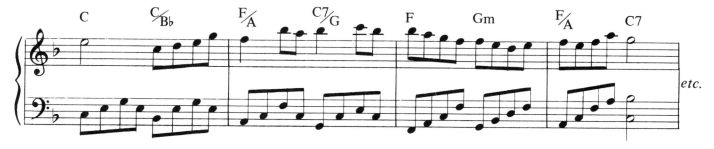

etc.

Notice how the bass line moves in a descending F major scale through the first four measures. In this realization we arpeggiated the chord, but the important bass notes are always on the strong beats. Notice the scalar movement is not interrupted. With a long, unidirectional bass line like this, it is important to start high enough if the line is descending, and low enough if the line is ascending. If we had started this tune an octave lower, the chords would be muddy sounding by the time we reached the F in the fourth measure. (If we tried to correct this by switching to a higher octave mid-way, the line of the bass would be broken.)

Unfortunately, not all fake charts are specific when indicating chord inversions, especially the charts intended for guitar accompaniment. Playing inversions when not specifically indicated will come naturally with experience. As a general rule, any time you can use an inversion to make a bass line move stepwise, it will probably sound good.

However, reading voice leading from a chord chart goes far beyond the bass line (which is very easy to read from the slash chord system of notation). There are also *inner* voices that move in similar fashion.

Let's look at a progression in closed position that we have seen before: Cm - Cm+7 - Cm7 - Cm6. This progression appears in "My Funny Valentine," as well as in many other songs. Here the "fourth note" of these four-note chords forms a line descending by half steps. To begin that line, the first Cm chord needs to have its root doubled on top, so that we can get the inner movement C - B - Bb - A.

If we take the moving inner voice and put it in the bass, we get a different "reading" of the chords.

The effect here is a little different, because the line is more emphasized in the bass. However, the two examples have similar harmonic effects, and they frequently substitute for one another.

Now let's look at some other inner voice patterns that we should be able to read from chord charts. Below are the first eight measures of the samba "Brazil", as written in most fake books.

etc.

71

The basic "vamp" accompaniment of the tune is clear enough. The fifth of the G chord moves up to D# to make an augmented G chord, then moves up again to the E, which is the sixth of the G6.

You may notice that the third chord (G6) is missing its fifth, because that's the note that's been moving up. If we were arranging this piece for a band, that line would be kept in one instrument or section, and our piano playing must do likewise.

The second four measures are the same harmonic pattern as the first four, built around the ii (A minor, in G) chord. We start on the A minor chord and move the top voice up and down (E - F - F# - F - E).

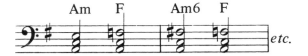

Let's look at another tune in which we have to "extract" the voice leading. Here are the first eight measures of "Embraceable You."

Realization:

The first two measures of our realization have an inner voice that goes in a direction opposite to the melody. Notice what happens in measures 3-4. The left hand has an ascending line that is harmonized in thirds (D+F# - E+G - F+Ab - F#+A). It starts and ends on a D7 chord, and the whole "feel" of measures 3 and 4 is D7. If one were to be very accurate, the second chord might be indicated as C/E, but this notation is typical of what you're going to find in some fake books.

The third chord of this voice leading group could be written as a Fm6 or a D#, depending on whether you are holding the C note from the previous bar. (We hold it over in our suggested realization, but it is not essential to this pattern.)

The fifth and sixth measures also have a voice leading example. Here, the E of the A min chord in the right hand moves up a half step (through the rest) to F, and then another half step to F#, while the lower A stays put, forming the F major and D7 chords respectively. This is a more sophisticated way of going through these changes, although there would be nothing wrong in playing them in root position.

Measures 7 and 8 contain a pattern similar to 3 and 4, but here the ascending line is on the G chord, rather than the D chord. Again, there is a double note ascending harmonization that can be figured out from the chord symbols.

You can see by now that these little "passing" harmonies are where fake books tend not to be satisfactory. In regular sheet music scores, the desired pattern is visually apparent, but in fake books we have to draw from our experience to figure out what is really intended. One good hint: we can often play such a "passing chord" pattern when the melody is static and the chord symbols start and end on the same chord. In such cases, a harmonic fill like those in the examples above is usually indicated. We can create our own voice leading from a chart that only gives the basic outline chords. This can entail using inversions to create a bass line and using passing inner harmonies as harmonic fills within a main chord. Let's take a simple chord chart and try a few examples of this.

Realization:

This tune is a rather standard progression of dominant seventh chords. The first two measures, having one chord per measure and a held melody note, are good examples of where to use moving harmonic lines to create a "fill" within a static melody. Here the player is "filling" on his own without any specific indication on the chord chart. Measure four has a little fill with the bass voice walking up in whole steps and the inner voices moving down in half steps. This figure is quite useful when a section to be repeated begins and ends on a I chord.

When we repeat the whole phrase (measures 5-8), we use the first inversion of the D chord (D/F#) so that the bass line moves linearly stepwise from F to F#, and then continues ascending from G to E. We use more exotic harmonies above this walking bass, but *the overall sound of measures 7 and 8 is still G7 to C7.* (Diminished chords are very useful in creating voice leading patterns where passing chords are used to harmonize a walking bass line.)

The bridge of this tune (measures 9-12) is a repeated two-measure phrase. The first time we keep the F in the bass for the B dim chord, so that it can walk up a whole tone to the Gm7 bass note. (Remember, diminished chords are usually not "fussy" about which chord tone is the bass note, as long is it has some relationship to the chord to which it moves.) By using Ab in the bass for the same chord two measures later, we create smooth voice leading. (If we used D in the bass it would also sound fine.) The only chord tone which would create weak voice leading would be the B itself. (Try playing just the bass notes of this change with the different voice leading possibilities and you will hear what I mean.)

Notice also in measures 11 and 12 how we use the first inversion of F to create nice voice leading in the bass of A - Ab - G, and then "walk" the bass up from C (C - D - E - F).

When the first phrase returns again (measures 13-16), we do something else in our voice leading. Here, instead of leading one or two voices into the next chord, we use a complete "upper neighbor" chord to slide down into the main chord. Notice how we use a quick Eb7 to slide into the D7, and an Ab7 to slide into the G7. The general guideline is that you can slide into a dominant seventh chord from the chord built a semi-tone higher.

We have now entered the subject area of embellishing the basic harmonic outline provided in the chord chart. Let us look at various ways to embellish this skeletal framework, both melodically and harmonically.

Embellishing and Varying the Accompaniment

Up until now, we have used notes that appear in the chords (chord tones) to provide our accompaniment to the melody. To add variety, we can frequently connect our chord tones with neighboring notes that don't belong to the indicated chord. Generally, these notes that don't belong will be placed on weak beats, so that our strong beats will continue to outline and define our basic chords. Let's look at some typical ways this is done.

One application of such "passing" notes is in an arpeggiated pattern. Below we use them in a ballad tune.

* *passing tones*

Notice that in the arpeggiated G major chord in the first measure and in the B minor chord in the second measure, we add an A and a C respectively as "passing" tones on weak beats. These notes connect the root and the third of the chords, but are not part of the chords. They just give the accompaniment some scale-like (step-wise) movement for variety.

In the third measure, notice how the note B in the bass helps the C chord pass into the A minor chord. If we eliminate the arpeggiated notes, we have this figure:

passing bass notes

The B is not part of the C major or the A minor chords; it is a neighboring note connecting the two, making a nice bass line. The same figure is then repeated before the F chord; the G in the bass is the passing note. Again, the notes connecting the two different chords generally occur on a weak beat just before the new chord is to be played. (It is perfectly acceptable to use two passing tones in a row.)

We see in this example that non-chord tones can be used both to connect chord tones with a single chord in an arpeggiated or broken chord pattern, and also to connect one chord to another when in a progression. A question you may have is how do you know which notes "fit" and which don't, since we are no longer limiting ourselves to the prescribed notes of the chord. There is no answer to this question that meets all situations. If our chord changes are *diatonic* (limited to the "natural" chords of our key signature), then our passing or neighboring notes can always be taken from the scale of the key we are in. For instance, look at the bass line for a simple I-IV-V-I pattern in F major below.

Here the passing notes all are derived from the F major scale. However, it is also possible to use notes *not* in the F scale. Here is the same chord pattern using some chromatic (out-of-scale) notes.

One guide to using chromatic passing tones is: if they are a semi-tone above or below a chord tone and then resolve to that chord tone, they usually sound good. However, it is not a good idea to have *too* many non-chord tones in the accompaniment, because that may destroy the sense of the harmony. You will usually want to play the root of the chord (or the appropriate chord tone if inverting) on the downbeat in order to establish the basic harmony.

This principle of approaching chord tones by notes a semi-tone away is a good way to anticipate a chord change. Notice in our previous example that the Bb chord in measure 3 is preceded by a bass note a semi-tone below. Similarly, the F major chord following is approached from the E below, and the pattern continues for the rest of the example.

One of the secrets of creating a good, full accompaniment is to have a distinct bass line (as would be played by a bass instrument or bass section within an ensemble), and also to have enough full chords so that the harmony is filled out. In our previously used "oom-pah" accompaniment, we generally alternated a single note in the bass (most often the root or the fifth) with a chord higher up. As we start adding non-chord passing tones as part of the bass line, we will create situations where non-chord bass notes are harmonized against the chord. Isolated, these notes may seem discordant, but, in the context of the whole line or phrase, such passing harmonic conflicts will sound fine. Pedal use, phrasing and dynamic level all affect the ear's ability to make harmonic sense out of passing non-harmonic tones.

Of course, the more we try to create a distinct bass line, the more difficult it will become to play the chords fully with just the left hand. The right hand often has to help out with the accompaniment, while at the same time providing the melody.

At times, you will want to play only a single note bass line with the left hand, and provide all the harmony plus the melody with the right hand. This is preferable when a fast or very rhythmic bass line is desired. For instance, look at the 12-bar blues pattern in C below. Notice how the active bass line is played by itself, and the supporting harmonies are provided by the right hand.

This does not mean that the right hand must always play the entire harmony
when there is a rhythmic bass line. Adding chords with the left hand to a rhythmic
bass line is most easily done "in between" bass notes, that is, when the bass has a
rest or a held note. Again using a blues pattern in C, here is a left hand part that
uses chords above the bass line in such a manner.

It is also possible to use arpeggiated chord patterns, instead of just block chords, *in between* the bass line on bottom and the melody on top. Such a pattern weaves a midrange arpeggio with the melody, and generally works best with slow, lyrical melodies. The arpeggio forms a simple "counter melody" to the main melody. Here is an example.

Notice how the chord is arpeggiated just underneath the melody while the bass line is well below. This gives the tune a full "three layer" sound. The middle part of such patterns, can, of course, be partially played with the left hand when convenient. If the rhythm of the melody gets too complex or moves too fast, it may be better to drop (or cheat on) the arpeggiated accompaniment for a moment. The bass line alone can carry the tune sufficiently for a short time. No one will notice anything is missing, because the rhythm will be continued. Try this pattern on a ballad of your own choosing. You will notice that the melody has to be played mainly with the fourth and fifth fingers of the right hand, so that the first three fingers are free to create the arpeggiation underneath. Practice slowly so that the interweaving is smooth.

By now, you may be getting the feeling that there is an endless variety of accompaniment possibilities. If you are looking for simple, inflexible rules, there are none. But having an infinite variety of possibilities is what makes music endlessly fresh and exciting.

Let us break our whole musical texture down into three elements: melody, bass and chord. Keeping these three elements in mind, let's look at some examples using the same tune and chord pattern.

In the first example, we use the oom-pah left hand, with the melody in the right. Next, we reverse the second oom-pah ("pah-oom"), so we have bass-chord-chord-bass. This creates quite a different rhythmic feel. In example three, we have a single note bass in the left hand, and an answer to the melody with chords in the right. This produces an interesting cross rhythm between the hands. In example four, we put the bass notes on the weak beat, which creates a syncopated, raggy feel (notice that the first bass note, G, is the fifth of the C chord). In example five, we break the chord into an eighth note pattern, the bottom note of each chord providing the implied bass line. (Making a clear distinction between a bass line and the rest of the harmonic accompaniment is not always possible or necessary, especially in arpeggiated or broken chord patterns. In example five, accenting the quarter-note beats would help bring out the bass.) In example six, the chords after the strong beat bass notes are played alternately by the left and right hands. Such an accompaniment utilizes a lot of the keyboard, and this helps create a full orchestral sound. In the last example, we have an arpeggiated accompaniment figure that doesn't seem to have a separate bass line, but by accenting certain notes (as shown) we can discern one.

We have now seen that we can embellish and vary our accompaniments by using non-harmonic notes (neighboring and passing notes), and various rhythmic and textural patterns. Let's try to put some of these ideas together in a tune.

Realization:

Note in this example how we play the bass line in octaves, giving it a full sound. We use chromatic passing notes to get from one chord to another several times (as in measures 2-3). When the left hand is playing a single bass note, the right fills in the chord; when the left plays more fully, the right can "lay back" and play less.

In the next example, the folk song "House of the Rising Sun," we have an arpeggiated accompaniment which uses some passing notes. This makes the arpeggiation more interesting and melodic. Remember, in this kind of pattern, we usually put the non-chord tones on weak beats, so they don't noticeably conflict with the harmony.

Note that in the last measure we don't use the arpeggiation pattern, but, rather, we walk down the E minor scale to get back to the I chord. This "turn-around" figure works well on phrases that end on a V or V7 chord. Try to work out this song with various other arpeggio patterns of your own.

Embellishing and Varying a Melody; Creating Counter Melody and Improvising Melodies

19

There are several reasons why we embellish the melody. The first is that it helps to change a song the second time around, so that our listeners do not get bored. Another reason is that a simple melody, especially one that is slow moving, may sound sparse in a solo piano arrangement. A singer or a wind instrumentalist can take a note and bend it, change its quality and make it vibrate. A pianist can't do much with a note once it's been struck. Finally, by embellishing the melody we can fill in "dead spots" (places where the melody rests), and prevent the music from losing continuity.

Grace notes, trills, arpeggios and tremolos are among the devices that can provide accent and flair to melodies. (By the way, such unwritten melodic embellishment was once a large part of the Baroque tradition). If over done, however, such ornamentation can get corny sounding. Below, we embellish the first four measures of "Swanee River."

One problem in making a melody work on the piano is in finding something to do with sustained notes. Even if they are sustained with the pedal, most notes die out fairly quickly. A good solution to this problem is to double the melody in octaves and roll the octave in a *tremolo*. This way you can maintain or increase the volume while sustaining the note. Below we demonstrate this technique.

tremolo marking

Notice that playing the melody in octaves gives it a much stronger effect. It is possible to fill out the sound even more by filling in the chord tones (completely or partly) within the octave.

One special kind of grace note is the "slip" note, used in much country-flavored music. A slip note "slips" into a chord tone from a neighboring suspended note. It is struck on the beat with the other notes before it goes to its resolution. With major chords, this device often goes from the second of the chord up to the third, or from the sixth down to the fifth; minor chords often have this grace note slipping from the seventh up to the root. The "slip" note can be used to embellish the melody; you can also add another chord tone on top of the melody for that real steel guitar sound! Here is an example.

Realization:

Note: Strike grace note on beat with other notes. Numbers refer to tones used for "slip."

Adding small embellishments to a melody is fine, but how else can we create more interesting music? One way is through a counter melody. This is a secondary melody which interweaves with the main tune, or fills in when the main tune pauses. An arpeggiated chord pattern, particularly if it appears above a separate bass line, can often be seen as a simple counter melody. (This is most applicable when the arpeggio fills in dead spots in the melody.) A more sophisticated counter melody will have the same attributes of any good melody; a mixture of different intervals, change of direction, and rhythmic variety. (Since counter melodies tend to be short phrases, great complexity is not always possible or desirable.) Counter melodies can add real style to your arrangements, making them sound more orchestral.

Some obvious questions are: "How does one go about spontaneously creating a counter melody?" "What notes are the 'right' ones?" and "Where and when can we fit them in?"

The last question is the easiest to answer. Any dead spot (a rest or long note in the melody) is the most likely place for a counter melody. Counter melody most often occurs just underneath the main melody, but it can also be played above (like the piccolo in marching band arrangements), or as a bass solo which diverges from the more regular and chord-oriented bass.

The simplest way to create a counter melody (one that goes beyond chord arpeggios) is to use the scale from which the chord is derived. We can't go wrong using our key scale (the F scale in the key of F, for example) as the basic source for our counter melody. We will want to use enough chord tones to help outline the harmony, so using a chord arpeggio as the framework for our counter melody is also a good idea. We will want to vary intervals and direction; a good counter melody never just runs up and down mechanically. Let's apply these ideas and create a counter melody.

Below is a melody line that lends itself to counter melody. Working with the first three measures, let's form an arpeggio for each chord, using an inversion which fits comfortably under the melody line.

Next, we use notes that neighbor these chord tones (derived from our basic F major scale) to fashion a short melodic phrase. Below is one possibility. The numbers indicate the chord tones used and the asterisks indicate neighboring tones and passing tones which come from, or resolve to, chord tones.

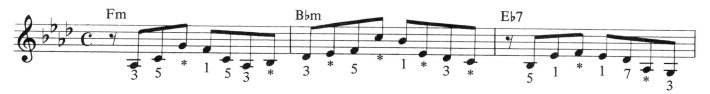

Now let's add this counter melody to our bass and main melody.

When creating your own melodies, either as counter melodies or as improvised variations to the main melody, you can add more "spice" by going outside of the diatonic scale and using some chromatic notes. You can often do this even if the chord changes themselves have no chromatic alterations. For instance, here is a simple melody that uses chromatic neighboring notes in the counter melody.

Realization: melody up an octave.

There are three special scales that are useful in certain situations for melodic fills or improvised variations. One is the "whole tone" scale, which comprises six whole steps (instead of the normal diatonic seven). It can be used as a run or a fill with a dominant chord with an altered (flat or sharp) fifth, and it creates a spacey, impressionistic effect. There are only two combinations of notes for whole tone scales. Another special scale is the diminished scale, which, not surprisingly, can be used with diminished chords. This scale alternates whole steps and half steps, giving us an eight-note scale, with three different combinations of notes (as with diminished seventh chords). Here are these two scales.

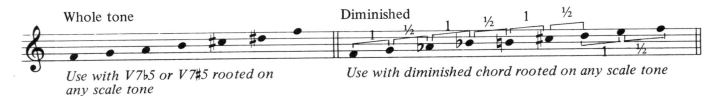

Whole tone
Use with V7♭5 or V7♯5 rooted on any scale tone

Diminished
Use with diminished chord rooted on any scale tone

Our final special scale is the blues scale, used not only with blues, but also with blues-influenced jazz, pop and rock. Remember, blues in its most basic form uses mostly dominant chords in the I, IV and V. The blues scale will flat the seventh and sometimes flat the third. A sharp fourth will also often appear. Melodies and accompaniment patterns based on this scale give a special, unmistakable sound that is very effective in many pop and rock tunes. Below is a blues scale in C.

Blues scale

I7   IV7   V7

Learning to embellish on the basic melody will take some work on your part, but coming up with a truly personal, original rendition of a tune will be very exciting and rewarding. It is helpful not to initially stray too far from the basic melody. As you get more comfortable with a tune, your experimentation can become more ambitious. Improvising original melodic ideas becomes especially important when we are accompanying a singer or solo instrumentalist, because, in these cases, we need not play the main melody at all. Our chief function in that case is to provide interesting interplay and tasteful support for the soloist. This brings us to our next chapter.

Accompanying a Singer or Soloist from a Fake Book

Almost everyone who plays the piano has had the experience of being at a party where someone wants to sing, and of being asked to accompany. Our first reaction may be to try to play the song exactly as if we were performing it solo. However, the playing that sounds best when someone else is singing or playing the melody can be quite different.

Generally, the accompaniment does not double the melody, except where specifically desired for emphasis. This does not mean that you do not have to look at the melody line and only have to pay attention to the chords. It is important to be aware of the rhythmic character of the melody to support it properly. Knowing where the melody is busy and where it is not is essential in order to put fills and accents in good spots. You may wish to play a line in harmony with the melody, or one that creates a counterpoint to it. You must know where the dramatic "peaks" and "valleys" of the song are. Although an accompanist doesn't necessarily play the melody, he or she must always listen to it and anticipate where it is going.

Now you are no longer responsible for the melody, which greatly expands your possibilities. For example, you can play full block chords in the right hand over a left hand bass line, or arpeggiated chords. Below are two examples using the chord change G-Am7-Bm7-C.

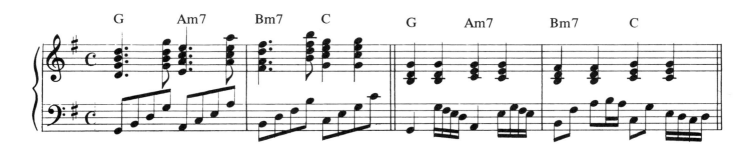

Notice that in the first version our block chords are varied by being inverted. The dotted note figure of the block chords provides rhythmic impetus. In the second version, the bass line provides the main interest while the right hand is fairly static and regular.

We could also reverse the order and put the block chords in the left hand while playing arpeggios or melodic figures in the right.

The second example is a pretty busy melody and it would probably work best as a fill while the primary melody is static.

Whatever chord pattern we use for our accompaniment (be it block chords, broken chords, arpeggios or counter melody), it is a good idea to vary the pattern to avoid monotony. Changing the inversions, the rhythm, the range of the keyboard you are using, the chord voicings—especially when there is a new phrase or section—are a few ways to create variety. With the right hand free from playing the melody, there is more opportunity to accentuate the rhythm. It can simply double the rhythm of the bass line, as in the example below, where the right hand plays chords in rhythmic unison with the left hand.

Or, to create a more complex rhythm, the left and right hands can interplay with more syncopation than one hand could do alone, as seen in this rock example.

A good accompanist strives to work from the vocal line. When the melody contains a lot of movement, it is usually best to accompany sparsely, using simple patterns. When there is space for a melodic fill by the accompanist, it is often effective to "echo" or imitate in some way the melody that preceded it. It is not necessary to play on every beat, or even in rhythmic unison with the melody; long sustained chords work well for many songs. Similarly, the accompanist does not have to play all the chord tones; the melody itself can provide some of them that need not be restated.

Let's see how we might apply some of these ideas to accompanying a well-known tune, "When the Saints Go Marching In."

ascending arpeggios

8va

"fill"

walking bass

countermelody

8va

2nd inversion creates nice bass line.

The top staff shows the melody and chords as they would appear in a fake book, and the bottom two staves represent a piano arrangement that could be used to accompany the melody. The left hand is playing our standard "oom-pah" broken chord arrangement, alternating the root and the fifth in the bass. Occasionally, there is a little "walking" bass (as in measures 7 and 11) to break the monotony. The right hand plays several familiar patterns: broken chords, arpeggios and block chords. We use little counter melodies that answer the vocal phrase at resting points (measures 2, 4, 8, 12-13 and 16). Notice in particular the effectiveness of leaping up an octave to play the "bluesy" fill in measure 8, and of using the high melody in octaves at the end. (If you also saw the bit of diminished scale, used in measure 13 for the B diminished chord, give yourself a gold star!)

These are just a few suggestions for improvising an accompaniment from a fake chart. Obviously, you have to be sensitive to your soloist in regard to tempo, dynamics, etc. A weak singer may need you to double the melody more often (at least to begin a phrase) so he or she can find the note; this is less a problem with an instrumentalist. When accompanying a whole group of amateur singers (in a sing-along situation), you will probably have to bang out the melody quite strongly to keep the group together. In such situations, you obviously have less opportunity for subtlety. The more skilled your soloist, the more chance you will have to create an inventive accompaniment.

Intros, Turn-arounds, and Endings

21

When beginning a song, it sometimes helps to use an introduction based on the last two or four measures of the tune. (This is particularly useful when people are singing along, because it helps them get started.) For instance, if we were going to play "He's Got the Whole World in His Hands," we could use this introduction:

Notice how the "walking" bass figure (D-E-F#) leads right into the opening G chord as the tune begins. This bass "pickup" is an easy formula you can always use —just walk up the scale from the fifth. (This assumes that the first chord of the tune is the I chord, which is true a great deal of the time.)

A few chords that just go around in a circle can help begin the song by establishing the key and getting the rhythm going. These are universal introductions (or "vamps") that can be applied to many songs, especially upbeat numbers. Following is a typical example, in the key of F. It is based on a simple four chord progression (I-VI7-iim7-V7), and could be repeated endlessly until you wanted to begin the tune. Transpose this intro to different keys, and try using it for such peppy tunes as "All of Me" or "Bye Bye Blackbird."

There are many ways to vary this kind of "vamp" intro using different chords. The melodies played with the chords can be of your own invention, you can use part of the real melody, you can use a completely different melody as a gag, or you can play chords with no real melody on top. Here are a few possibilities for this type of intro, with the chords indicated by Roman numerals, as well as letter names (to help you transpose to other keys). See if you can use these formulas and make up some of your own as well.

Of course, the specific choice of intro depends on the rhythm and tempo of the tune and the mood you want to create. With a slow ballad, often a simple arpeggio on the dominant seventh chord (the V7 chord), perhaps in the augmented (#5) form, can effectively "set up" the entrance of the melody. Tunes like "Misty" or "Days of Wine and Roses" easily follow such a chord.

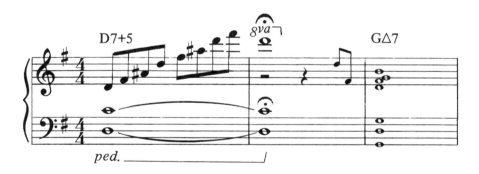

When you finish playing a song and you intend to repeat it, you want to avoid a sense of finality, so you have to keep playing after you reach the last melody note and chord. It's acceptable to just "vamp" on the final chord of the tune for a measure or two, keeping the rhythm going, but it's better to use other lead-in chords, as we did for our intros. If the song begins on the I chord, we could throw in a quick V7 or use a IIm7-V7 progression to create the sense of starting over. For instance, if we were playing "Home on the Range" in D, we could play a one measure Em7-A7 after the final D, before starting again at the head. This is called a "turnaround."

If a tune begins on a chord other than the I, a chord or progression which will lead back to that opening chord can similarly be used. For instance, if our song opens on the ii chord (as do "Satin Doll," "Body and Soul," and countless others), a dominant seventh on VI (which is the V of ii chord) can serve as the "pivot."

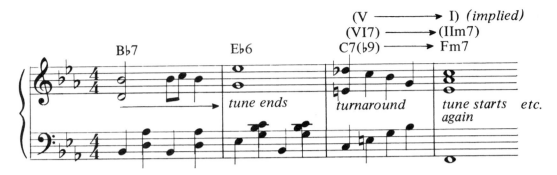

A variation of this is to use a diminished chord a semitone below to lead in to the minor ii chord.

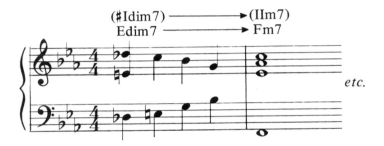

Sometimes it can be a little tricky to end a tune, especially since so many contemporary pop recordings end with a "fade out." In such situations, sometimes a *"ritard"* (slowing down) will help bring a sense of finality to the last chords. For example, if we were to end "Arthur's Theme," in which the last measure of each chorus wants to go back to the next verse, we can close things with a final dramatic ritard. Here we demonstrate such an ending in D (using a cadence reminiscent of gospel music), which starts on the IV chord and "walks down" to the final chord.

When professional pianists play standards, they often use certain harmonic figures for the ending to give it more flair and style than it would otherwise have. Many of these formulas are called "deceptive cadences." A cadence is a resting point in music. In a deceptive cadence, you expect to hear a final, resolved I chord, but some other chord is used as a substitute, delaying the final resolution. There are number of different deceptive cadences that can be used as slick, stylish endings. One such cadence uses chords that are built on neighbor notes to the tonic —a semi-tone above or below (the VIIΔ7 or bIIΔ7). For instance, if we were ending a song in G, we could delay the final chord with an Ab or F# chord, or a combination of both. As demonstrated below, these endings generally work best in tunes that do not use simple triads, but contain richer harmonies (major and minor sixths, sevenths, etc.).

Besides using a major seventh chord as our neighbor deceptive cadence chord, we can use a major sixth or a dominant seventh chord (bII6, bII7, VII6, VII7). The effect is similar, but we should choose a chord type to accommodate particular notes that are repeated or sustained, or one that will mirror a particular melodic figure. (In our example, there is an A held in the last bar, and the chords used [B7, A6] also contain that note.)

There are other good deceptive cadence chords besides those which lie a semi-tone away from the tonic. These also may be used in combinations or by themselves. A major chord built a full tone below the I (the bVII chord in a major key) is often used, sometimes "walking up" chromatically to the I, or skipping up to the II before the final chord resolves.

Also possible is the *b*VI, a major chord built a major third below the I. This deceptive cadence is especially effective with a sustained note at the end when that note is a common tone for both the *b*VI and the I chord. (For instance, the note C held for the final note of a song in C is part of both the deceptive A*b* major chord and the final C major chord.) The *b*VI can have a subtle effect when combined with other passing chords, but when used along with the *b*VII, also creates a big climactic ending (as shown below).

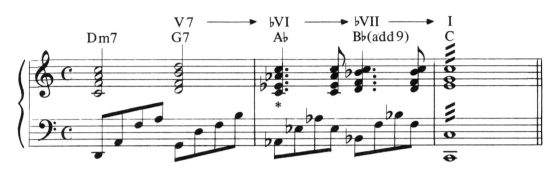

There are several longer and more sophisticated chord progressions that work equally well as deceptive endings or as introductions. We can't go into all of them, but one frequently used progression starts on a half-diminished chord built an augmented fourth (diminished 5th) above the I chord and then descends chromatically. Here is an example of this progression in B*b*; work it out in other keys as well. In this pattern, the chromatic bass line is the key element, while the specific chord type (major, minor, diminished, sixth, seventh, or ninth) can often be altered without much difference in effect.

Before we finish our discussion of endings and intros, we would be remiss if we did not mention a few favorite "cliché" tags that are used—often with humorous intent—to end a tune, particular light-hearted, peppy numbers. Practice transposing them so you can use them spontaneously in any key. The first one is the famous "Basie tag," often heard in big band swing arrangements.

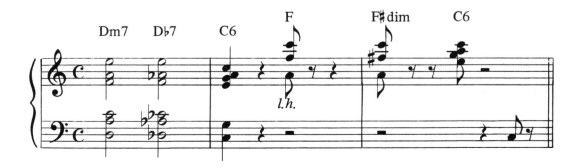

Another common tag line is based on the contrary motion of the treble and bass voices.

The above figure can be filled in harmonically for a "fatter" sounding version.

Another way to vary this is to switch the voices, so they move apart rather than together. Here we do this in F with a dotted rhythmic figure.

Last but not least, here is the "Shave and a Haircut" tag, always good for a chuckle from your listeners!

These are just a few ideas among infinite possibilities for intros, turnarounds, and endings. Listen to what other pianists do, and try always to be creative and invent your own!

Summary of Basic Accompaniment Patterns; Special Styles

22

You should be well started on your career as a "faker." If you work at it, you will be able to develop the ability to play a full and satisfying rendition of any tune at its first reading from a fake chart. More sophisticated stylizations (like those played by accomplished professional piano soloists) take longer to develop, but you now have a basic foundation on which you can continue to build.

Below is a collection of basic accompaniment styles for different types of tunes, shown with a few sample measures of each. Much of what is here is simply a review, so we can eliminate commentary in these cases. These patterns are not intended to be rigid formulas for accompaniments, but to be suggestions that you should vary and embellish, according to your taste and the particular requirements of different tunes. These basic patterns, and the variations you will create on your own, are sufficient to cover a great deal of popular music.

Marine's Hymn — March ($\frac{4}{4}$ time)

Pattern 1 — straight block chords (with rhythmic variation)

Pattern 2 — broken chords (with alternating 1-5 bass)

Pattern 3 — broken chord (with "walking" bass line)

Bill Bailey Swing Bass ($\frac{2}{4}$ or cut time — 2 accents per measure)

Pattern 1 — broken chord with alternating bass

Pattern 2 — broken chord with moving bass line

"walking bass"   or: arpeggiated chord

Pattern 3 — "stride" style

Slow Ballad (Duple or triple meter)

Gm   Cm7   F7   Bb△7

Pattern 1 — broken chord (open spacing)

Pattern 2 — eighth note arpeggios

space chord wide on bottom; close on top.

Pattern 3 — bass note—chord (only downbeat accented)

chords invert

Pattern 4 — bass —chord with moving bass line

Pattern 5 — "Classical" style (known as "Alberti Bass") in quarter notes

Pattern 6 — "Classical" style in eighth notes

"Swing" (Fast 4/4 — 4 accents...) *

* *Accenting every beat in a fast tempo can be problematic for solo piano. Sometimes it's better to relax the left hand and "imply" the pulse, accenting only the downbeat of each measure, as in pattern 1.*

Pattern 1

Pattern 2 — steady 4 block chords

Use light staccato touch. Notice inversions and stepwise motion facilitate playing.

Pattern 3 — single note bass line arpeggiating chord

Pattern 4 — single note bass line with passing notes (walking bass)

(Use full chording in right hand)

Waltz ($\frac{3}{4}$ time)

Pattern 1 — alternating bass with broken or block chords (oom-pah)

etc.

Pattern 2 — chord arpeggio

(Use pedal to sustain sounds of single notes through chord)

etc.

Pattern 3 — broken chord arpeggio

etc.

Pattern 4 — moving bass line with chords

Bass notes arpeggiate chord —

etc.

— or move stepwise

Pattern 5 — eighth note arpeggios

etc.

"Special" Styles and Patterns

Certain styles of music require a specific accompaniment to get the right "feel". The particular identifying characteristic may be rhythmic (as in Latin dance music), it may be harmonic (as in "cocktail" piano), or it may be a combination of both. Here are a few of these special accompaniment styles. You don't have to limit their use to the tunes for which they are named; a beguine accompaniment can be used on songs that are not known as beguines. It's fun to utilize a variety of musical styles in different contexts; the larger the stylistic "vocabulary" you can quote from, the more versatile you will be and the less monotonous your playing.

For most of these special styles you can use a "vamp" figure to begin the song. In this context, we can define a vamp as an introduction that sets up a particular rhythmic and/or harmonic pattern before the beginning of the melody. One question you may have is, "If I am using both hands just for the vamp (which is necessary for many syncopated rhythms) how the heck am I going to have enough fingers left over for the melody as well?" The answer is simply to "cheat" when necessary. If we have a recurring rhythmic pattern, the ear tends to continually hear it, even if we drop it to accommodate the melody. When the melody rests, we can return the accompaniment pattern to the right hand. In our first example, the beguine style, we give an example of this (in m. 4-5).

Notice how our vamp introduction, with the characteristic syncopation between the bass and the answering chords in the right hand, sets up the beguine rhythm. Where our melody comes in, in bars 4 and 6, those answering chords have to temporarily drop out. The bass continues its rhythm, while the right hand's counter rhythm returns when the melody rests in the following bar. The result is that it doesn't sound as if anything is missing!

The beguine rhythm and variations on it can be used for boleros and slow rhumbas, such as "Spanish Eyes," "What a Difference a Day Makes," "Magic is the

Moment," as well as many others. Two other variations on this basic Latin vamp are below.

A tango can be created with a dotted rhythm figure that uses a broken chord.

The tango pattern *must* contain: a downbeat root for a dotted quarter note, then the fifth for an eighth note, followed by the root and third together (an octave higher) for a quarter note, and the fifth again for a quarter note. If we have chords bigger than triads, we may alter the note placement as necessary, but the rhythm must stay the same.

Once we get comfortable with this pattern, we may add a counter rhythm in the right hand similar to that of the beguine. Again, when the melody is moving too fast, we will have to drop the separate rhythmic textures in the right hand. Notice that in this example we have used two different counter rhythms. Use either of these, or invent your own.

Another Latin rhythm is the Calypso. In this, the bass has three notes per measure, the first and second having a characteristic syncopation. A calypso bass vamp in C would look like this:

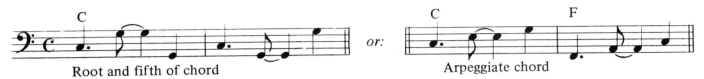

Root and fifth of chord   *or:*   Arpeggiate chord

As a vamp introduction to a calypso tune (such as "Yellow Bird"), we might play the bass line rhythmically doubled with block chords in the right hand. Once the melody begins, we may leave the rhythm to the left hand, and use the right hand for melody with harmonic support. (Calypsos sound good with simple harmonies in thirds and sixths, as demonstrated below.)

Another accompaniment style that can be used is the shuffle beat. A true shuffle beat has a 12/8 feel, with each quarter note being subdivided into a triplet. There are two bass notes on each quarter note beat, the first one taking up two-thirds of the beat and the second one taking up the remaining third. Note the difference between a shuffle rhythm and a regular dotted rhythm as shown below. The shuffle has a "lazier" sound than the dotted eighth/sixteenth figure.

In most instances, the shuffle will be written as a dotted figure, but should be played with a triplet feel. The shuffle rhythm can be used with quite a variety of bass figurations, achieving quite different effects. One of its most stereotyped uses is in Western music, where, typically, a sixth is added to the triad, as shown here:

A variation on this is to play a broken chord, as we did for the tango.

A different figure using a shuffle rhythm is used in quite a different type of music:

This is one of many blues patterns. (You may recall that in the basic blues pattern dominant sevenths are used on the I, IV, and V. This explains the G natural and C natural in the key of A.) Notice the pattern is an ascending and descending arpeggiation of the chord, with a passing note between the fifth and the seventh of each chord.

If we break up each beat into an octave, we get our classic "boogie-woogie" left hand:

The shuffle and boogie-woogie patterns represent just one kind of blues style. Rock-n-roll uses many of the same chord progressions but the rhythms can be different. Here is a simple pattern that could be used for accompanying rock-n-roll as well as other blues-derived genres. The important thing here is an accent on the off-beats 2 and 4 (the so-called "back beat" of rock).

* *chromatic passing tone*

There is one style of piano playing that is not based on rhythm at all; in fact, there is no rhythm in the accompaniment, except that dictated by the melody. We are referring to the "locked hands" cocktail style. This was popularized by the great jazz pianist George Shearing, and is frequently heard as background music in restaurants and/or as "easy listening" radio programming. The basic "trick" here is to double the melody an octave lower with the left hand and fill out the chord in between. Playing this style correctly often requires a sophisticated sense of harmony. Not only do you have to instantly invert the chords to fit within the octave, but you must utilize many harmonic substitutions for the written chords, such as passing chords (especially diminished chords), as well as fancy voice leading. The chords used in this style would generally be sevenths and larger, often with unusual voicings. In other words, this is not a style to use for "Oh Susanna," unless Susanna has moved to the big city and taken to drinking white wine spritzers!

For those who would like to attempt this style, here is an example of how it works. Let's use the famous theme from Chopin's "Fantasie-Impromptu" (later used as the melody for "I'm Always Chasing Rainbows").

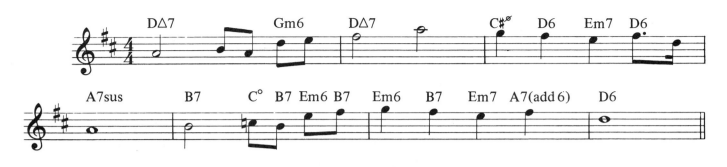

Realization:

Notice that in this arrangement we don't use plain triads. Our D chord becomes a D6 or Dmaj7; the Em becomes Em6 or Em7. The left hand plays the melody alone while the right hand plays the rest of the chord plus the melody on top. (It would be possible to distribute the notes more evenly between the hands, but this is usually the easiest approach.) Facility in this style will take a lot of practice; at first it's best to work with slower melodies so the fingers can find the right notes. To get used to playing the melody in the left hand will also take much practicing, but facility in that skill will give you "chops" that can be put to gratifying uses in other styles as well.

We have covered just a few of the styles of popular music; it would be impossible to develop each in detail within one book. With some work on your part you should be able to play like a "pro," not depending on written sheet music arrangements. As a result, your playing will develop more life and spontaneity. If you aren't struggling to read notes, both you and your listeners can get more immediate pleasure from your music. (There is no reason why your arrangement of a pop tune can't be as good as, or better than, a published arrangement!)

The best rule of thumb in music is always this: *if it sounds good to you, it is good.* Do a lot of sight reading, experiment with various accompaniments, and try gradually to build up your personal repertoire of tunes that you can play from memory. The more you play each tune and become familiar with it, the more new ideas you will find yourself adding. Good luck, and good music!

Glossary

Alternate Spellings — See "Enharmonics"

Arpeggiate — To play the notes of a chord in rapid succession. Often used as an accompaniment pattern.

Augmented — The largest interval quality. One forms an augmented interval by enlarging a major or perfect interval ½ step.

Augmented triad — This chord does not appear in any major scale, and only appears on the 3rd step of the harmonic minor scale, or the 3rd step of the *ascending* melodic minor scale. In root position, it is formed by superimposing a major third over another major third.

Chord — Three or more notes played simultaneously.

Chromatic — Any of the symbols, #, b, ♮, ✕, bb. Also, any note which is not found in the key signature, and is preceded by one of the above symbols. (i.e. Ab would be a chromatic note in the key of C Major.)

Chromatic scale — A scale of twelve half steps.

Close position — See chapter IX, paragraph 3.

Compound interval — Intervals larger than an octave. They are the ninth (octave + 2nd), the tenth (octave + 3rd), the eleventh (octave + 4th), the twelfth (octave + 5th), and the thirteenth (octave + 6th).

Deceptive Cadence — A chord, or series of chords, which delay the resolution from dominant chord to tonic chord. Usually, they are bII, bVI, bVII, or VII chords, or a combination thereof.

Diatonic — Any unaltered notes appearing in a given scale. If a note is raised or lowered by ½ step or 1 whole step, it becomes a *chromatic* note (see "chromatic").

Diminished interval — The smallest interval. One forms a diminished interval by making a minor or a perfect interval ½ step smaller.

Diminished scale — A scale comprising nine notes, alternating whole steps and half steps.

Diminished triad — This chord is, in root position, two superimposed minor thirds, and can be found on the 7th scale tone in a major key and the 2nd scale tone in a minor key.

Dominant seventh — See chapter XI

Duple meter — Music having two beats per measure, the first being stronger than the second, is said to be in duple meter.

Enharmonics — Two or more notes that have the same pitch, but different letter names (i.e., D✕ , E & Fb are the same note, as are C, B# and Dbb).

Grace note — A non-harmonic note which is generally played before the beat, resolving immediately in step-wise motion to a chord tone.

Intervals — The distance between two notes. The intervals are: seconds, thirds, fourths, fifths, sixths, sevenths, octaves, ninths, tenths, elevenths, twelfths, and thirteenths. The intervals larger than an octave are called *compound intervals*.

Inversions — A motion which is used to describe chords and intervals. If one takes the lowest note of a chord or interval and moves it above the other members of that chord (or interval), one is said to have *inverted* it.

Lead sheet — A single piece of music presented in fake book form.

Major interval — Used to define intervallic quality. The intervals which can be major are the 2nd, 3rd, 6th and 7th. In a major key, the distance from the root to the 2nd, 3rd, 6th and 7th is a major interval. To make these intervals ½ step smaller would make them minor intervals; to make them ½ step larger would make them augmented.

Major scale — A succession of 8 notes, the intervals between the notes being in the following order: step, step, ½ step, step, step, step, ½ step.

Major Sixth and Seventh — See Chapter XI.

Major triad — A three note chord. In root position, it is a minor third superimposed over a major third. This triad appears diatonically on the 1st, 4th and 5th steps of a major scale, and the 3rd, 6th and 7th steps of the natural minor scale.

Meter — The number of beats in one measure of music. There are duple (2 beats), triple (3 beats), and quadruple (4 beats) meters, as well as compound meters (i.e., quintuple is a combination of duple and triple).

Minor interval — An interval which is ½ step smaller than a major interval. The intervals which can be minor are the 2nd, 3rd, 6th and 7th. To make these intervals ½ step smaller would make them diminished; to enlarge them ½ step would make them major.

Minor scale — There are 3 minor scales: natural, harmonic and melodic. The natural uses the following interval pattern: 1, ½, 1, 1, ½, 1, 1

The harmonic minor is the natural minor with the 7th scale tone raised ½ step. It follows this intervallic pattern:
1, ½, 1, 1, ½, 1½, ½
The melodic minor has a raised 6th and 7th when ascending; these two scale tones are lowered when descending. Here are the melodic minor's ascending and descending intervals:
1, ½, 1, 1, 1, 1, ½   Ascending
l, ½, 1, 1, ½, 1, 1   Descending

Minor 6ths and 7ths — See chapter XII

Minor triad — A three note chord which appears diatonically on the 2nd, 3rd and 6th steps of any major scale, and the 1st, 4th and 5th steps of the natural minor scale. It is, in root position, a major third superimposed over a minor third.

Non-harmonic tones — Any note that is not found in a chord or a key. In a C major scale, a D# is a chromatic non-harmonic tone. In a C major chord, a D would be a diatonic non-harmonic tone. Examples of non-harmonic tones are: neighbor tones, passing tones, grace notes.

Neighbor tones — Any note lying ½ step from another. Every note has two neighbors: an upper and a lower.

Open position — See chapter IX, paragraph No. 4.

Passing tones — Non-harmonic tones (either chromatic or diatonic) which connect two chord tones. They are usually on weak beats, but it is not too uncommon to see them on strong beats. Two passing tones may be strung together.

Pedal point — A note in the bass which is sustained underneath a chord progression. It is usually separated by the distance of at least an octave, and is not necessarily a chord tone for all the chords in the progression above it.

Perfect — This is an intervallic quality used only to define fourths, fifths and octaves. To enlarge this by ½ step would make an augmented interval; making it ½ step smaller would make it diminished.

Quadruple meter — Music having four beats per measure, the beats being alternately strong and weak, is said to be in quadruple meter.

Quality — Used in conjunction with intervals, quality further defines the size of an interval. (See also perfect, major, minor, diminished, and augmented)

Realization — The process by which one reads a fake chart and creates music from it.

Relative minor — If used to describe a key signature, the relative minor has the same key signature as the major key which begins a minor third above its root (the A minor scale uses the key signature for C major; the D minor scale uses the key signature for F major). If used to describe a minor scale, the relative minor scale begins on the 6th step of any major scale. (The relative minor of E♭ major is C minor, the relative minor of A♭ major is F minor.)

Ritard — Getting slower.

Scale — The unidirectional succession of notes within an octave. There are usually eight notes in a scale, although the whole tone scale has six, the chromatic has twelve, and the diminished has nine. The scales are: major, minor (natural, harmonic and melodic), diminished, whole tone and chromatic.

Slash chords — A chord symbol which specifies a bass note. (C/G would be a C major chord with a G as the bass note.)

Slip note — A grace note played on the beat, resolving immediately to a chord tone.

Syllables — In traditional music theory, each step of the scale (be it major or minor) is assigned a syllable. They are: do, re, mi, fa, sol, la, ti, do. In a chromatic scale, they are altered and become: do, di, re, ri, mi, fa, fi, sol, si, la, li, ti, and do.

Syncopation — The replacement of a strong beat with a weak one, and vice versa.

Tag — A short, distinctive phrase used at the end of a piece of music, often with humorous intent.

Taking off — A term used frequently by jazz musicians to mean free jazz improvisation.

Tremolo — The rapid repetition of two or more notes, producing a trembling effect.

Triad — Chords comprising three notes. There are four types of triads: major, minor, diminished and augmented. (See also major, minor, diminished and augmented triads.)

Trill — The rapid repetition of two notes which lie either a whole step apart or a half step apart.

Triple meter — Music having three beats per measure, the first beat being stronger than the second or third, is said to be in triple meter.

Tritone — An interval which bisects an octave. It comprises 3 whole tones, and is also known as an augmented fourth or a diminished fifth.

Turnaround — A short harmonic phrase used at the end of a tune to return it to the opening chord.

Vamp — A recurring harmonic or melodic pattern. If used as an introduction to a tune, it establishes the characteristic rhythm of that tune.

Voice leading — The manner in which a "voice" moves, creating a melody of its own within a piece of music. Generally, "good" voice leading is said to move in step-wise motion.

Whole tone scale — A scale comprising six notes, the interval between all scale tones being a whole step.

Glossary of Symbols and Chords

 # - sharp—If put in front of a note, raise that note ½ step. (D# is one half step higher than D natural)

b - flat—If placed in front of a note, lower that note ½ step. (Db is one half step lower than D natural)

bb - double flat—If put in front of a flatted note, lower that note ½ step. (Dbb is ½ step lower than Db)

✕ - double sharp—If put in front of a previously sharped note, raise that note another ½ step. (D ✕ is ½ step higher than D#)

4/4 four beats per measure; quarter note gets the beat

3/4 three beats per measure; quarter note gets the beat

2/4 two beats per measure; quarter note gets the beat

These are the three most common time signatures. All time signatures are read the same way. The upper number tells the number of beats per measure, and the bottom number tells what kind of note gets a beat.

C - common time—This is the same as 4/4 time.

¢ - cut time—This is written as if it were 4/4 time, but it is played as if it were 2/4 time (it is played twice as fast as 4/4 time).

min, m, - (rare)—Used to indicate a minor triad. (i.e., Cmin)

aug, +—Used to indicate an augmented triad. (i.e., Caug, C+)

dim., o—Used to indicate a diminished triad. (i.e., C°, Cdim)

ø—Used to indicate a half diminished seventh chord. Formed by adding a minor seventh to a diminished triad. (i.e., C, Eb, Gb Bb)

△7, Maj7, ma7, M7—Used to indicate a major seventh chord. Formed by adding a major seventh to a major triad.

6, add 6—Used to indicate a major sixth chord. Formed by adding a major sixth to a major triad. (i.e., C, E, G, A)

7—Used to indicate a dominant seventh chord. Formed by adding a minor seventh to a major triad. (i.e., C, E, G, Bb)

min6, m6, - 6—Used to indicate a minor sixth chord. Formed by adding a minor sixth to a minor triad. (i.e., C, Eb, G, Ab)

min7, m7, -7—Used to indicate a minor seventh chord. Formed by adding a minor seventh to a minor triad. (i.e., C, Eb, G, Bb)

min(maj7), - (△7), min#7, min ♮7, min+7—Used to indicate a minor triad with an added major seventh. (i.e., C, Eb, G, B)

dim7, °7—Used to indicate a diminished seventh chord. Formed by adding a diminished 7th to a diminished triad. (i.e., C, Eb, Gb, Bbb)

7aug5, aug7, 7(+5), 7(#5), +7, 7+—Used to indicate a dominant seventh with an altered fifth. Formed by raising the fifth of a dominant seventh chord ½ step. (i.e., C, E, G#, Bb)

-5, b5—Used to indicate a dominant 7th with an altered fifth. Formed by lowering the fifth of a dominant seventh chord ½ step. (i.e., C, E, Gb, Bb)

sus4, sus2, 4, 2, sus9, 9th no 7th—Used to indicate suspended chords. In the "sus4" or "4" chord, a fourth will be substituted for the third of any seventh chord or triad. In the "sus2," "2," "sus9," or "9th no 7th" chords, the 2nd (or 9th) is in addition to the root and the third. This chord will *not* have a 7th.

9—Used to indicate a dominant ninth chord. Formed by adding a major 9th to a dominant 7th chord. (i.e., C, E, G, Bb, D)

9(b5), 9(-5)—Used to indicate a dominant 9th with an altered fifth. Formed by lowering the 5th of a dominant 9th chord ½ step. (C, E, Gb, Bb, D)

9(#5), 9(+5), aug9—Used to indicate a dominant 9th with an altered fifth. Formed by raising the fifth of a dominant ninth chord by ½ step. (i.e., C, E, G#, Bb, D)

min9, - 9—Used to indicate a minor ninth chord. Formed by adding a major 9th to a minor seventh chord. (i.e., C, Eb, G, Bb, D)

maj9, △ 9, M9—Used to indicate a major ninth chord. Formed by adding a major 9th to a major seventh chord. (i.e., C, E, G, B, D)

maj9(no 3rd)—Used to indicate a specific voicing of a major 9th chord. (i.e., C, G, B, D)

7b9—Used to indicate an altered dominant seventh chord. Formed by adding a minor ninth to a dominant 7th chord. (i.e., C, E, G, Bb, Db)

7#9, min/maj, 7(add min 3)—Used to indicate an altered dominant seventh chord. Formed by adding an augmented 9th to a dominant seventh chord (the aug. 9th is the enharmonic equivalent of the minor third). (i.e., C, E, G, Bb, D#)

7b5#9—Used to indicate an altered dominant seventh chord. Formed by adding a diminished fifth and an augmented ninth to a dominant seventh chord. (i.e., C, E, Gb, Bb, D#)

7b5b9—Used to indicate an altered dominant seventh chord. Formed by adding a diminished fifth and a minor ninth to a dominant seventh chord. (i.e., C, E, Gb, Bb, Db)

7#5#9—Used to indicate an altered dominant seventh chord. Formed by adding an augmented fifth and an augmented ninth to a dominant seventh chord. (i.e., C, E, G#, Bb, D#)

7#5b9—Used to indicate an altered dominant seventh chord. Formed by adding an augmented fifth and a minor ninth to a dominant seventh chord. (i.e., C, E, G#, Bb, Db)

6/9—Used to indicate a major triad with added tones. Formed by adding a major sixth and a major ninth to a major triad. (i.e., C, E, G, A, D)

11—Used to indicate a dominant eleventh chord. Formed by adding the eleventh to a dominanat ninth chord. (i.e., C, E, G, Bb, D, F)

11b9—Used to indicate an altered dominant eleventh chord. Formed by adding a minor ninth and the eleventh to a dominant seventh chord. (i.e., C, E, G, Bb, Db, F)

13—Used to indicate a (dominant) thirteenth chord. Formed by adding a thirteenth to a dominant eleventh chord. It is usually voiced without the third or fifth. (i.e., Bb △7/C = C13 = C, (E), (G), Bb, D, F, A)

b9b13—Used to indicate an altered thirteenth chord. Formed by adding a minor ninth, eleventh and minor thirteenth to a dominant seventh chord. It is usually voiced without the third or fifth. (i.e., C, (E), (G), Bb, Db, F, Ab = Bbmin7/C = Cb9b13)

13b9—Used to indicate an altered thirteenth chord. Formed by adding a minor ninth to a dominant thirteenth chord. (i.e., C, (E), (G), Bb, Db, F, A)

23

After the Ball

By CHARLES K. HARRIS

After the ball is o - ver, Af - ter the break of dawn, After the danc - ers' leav - ing, Af - ter the stars are gone, Man - y a heart is ach - ing, If you could read them all Man - y the hopes that have van - ished, Af - ter the ball.

All Through the Night

1. Sleep, my child, and peace attend thee,
   All through the night;
   Guardian angels God will send thee,
   All through the night.
   Soft the drowsy hours are creeping,
   Hill and vale in quiet sleeping,
   I my loving vigil keeping,
   All through the night.

2. While the moon her watch is keeping
   All through the night;
   While the weary world is sleeping,
   All through the night.
   O'er thy spirit gently stealing,
   Visions of delight revealing,
   Breathes a pure and holy feeling,
   All through the night.

Alouette

FRENCH TRADITIONAL SONG

2. Alouette Gentile Alouette. Alouette je te plumerai.
    Je te plumerai la bec, Je te plumerai la bec.
    Et la tete, et la tete, et la tete, et la tete. Oh
    Alouette Gentile Alouette. Alouette je te plumerai.

Amazing Grace

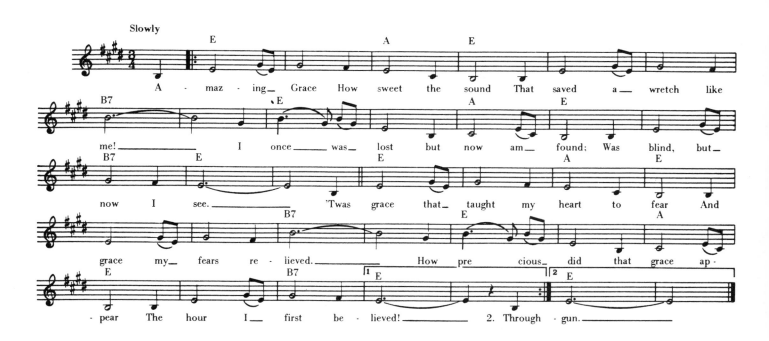

2. (Through) many dangers, toils and snares I have already come.
    'Tis grace hath brought me safe thus far, And grace will lead me home.
    When we've been there ten thousand years, Bright shining as the sun.
    We've no less days to sing God's praise Than when we first begun.

America

Words by
Rev. SAMUEL F. SMITH

My coun-try, 'tis of thee, Sweet land of lib-er-ty, Of thee I sing. Land where my fa-thers died, Land of the pil-grims pride, From ev-'ry___ moun-tain-side, Let___ free-dom ring.

The Ash Grove

1. Down yonder green valley, where streamlets meander,
   When twilight is fading I pensively rove;
   Or at the bright noon-tide, in solitude wander,
   Amid the dark shade of the lonely ash grove.
   'Twas there, while the blackbird was cheerfully singing,
   I first met that dear one, the joy of my heart!
   Around us for gladness the bluebells were ringing:
   Ah! then little thought I how soon we should part.

2. Still glows the bright sunshine o'er valley and mountain,
   Still warbles the blackbird its note from the tree;
   Still trembles the moonbeam on streamlet and fountain,
   But what are the beauties of nature to me?
   With sorrow, deep sorrow, my bosom is laden,
   All day I go mourning in search of my love!
   Ye echoes! oh, tell me, where is the sweet maiden?
   "She sleeps 'neath the green turf down by the ash grove".

America the Beautiful

By SAMUEL A. WARD

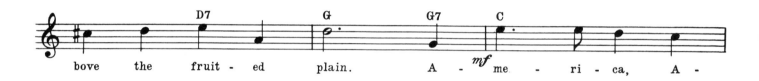

Aura Lee

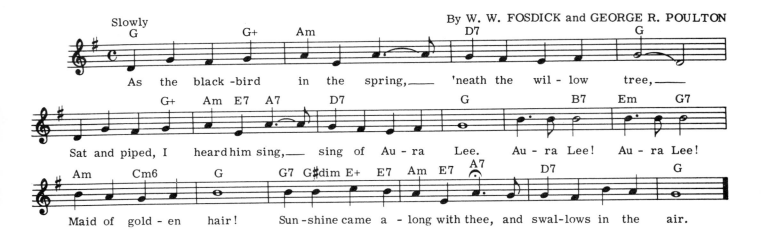

By W. W. FOSDICK and GEORGE R. POULTON

Slowly

As the black-bird in the spring,___ 'neath the wil-low tree,___ Sat and piped, I heard him sing,___ sing of Au-ra Lee. Au-ra Lee! Au-ra Lee! Maid of gold-en hair! Sun-shine came a-long with thee, and swal-lows in the air.

Auld Lang Syne

Words by ROBERT BURNS
Scottish Tune

Slowly

Should auld ac-quaint-ance be for-got and nev-er brought to mind, Should auld ac-quaint-ance be for-got, And___ days of auld lang syne. For auld___ lang___ syne, my dear, for auld___ lang___ syne, We'll take a cup o' kind-ness yet, For___ auld___ lang___ syne.

Ave Maria

By FRANZ SCHUBERT

Away in a Manger

By JAMES R. MURRAY

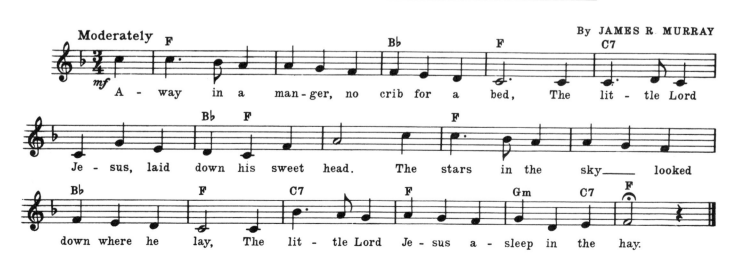

A - way in a man - ger, no crib for a bed, The lit - tle Lord Je - sus, laid down his sweet head. The stars in the sky___ looked down where he lay, The lit - tle Lord Je - sus a - sleep in the hay.

The Band Played On

By PALMER and WARD

Moderate Waltz

mf Ca - sey would waltz with a straw-ber - ry blonde, And the band played on. He'd glide 'cross the floor with the girl he a - dor'd, And the band played on. But his brain was so load-ed, it near-ly ex-plod-ed, The poor girl would shake with a - larm. He'd ne'er leave the girl with the straw-ber - ry curl, And the band played on.

Beautiful Isle of Somewhere

by JESSIE BROWN POUNDS & JOHN S. FEARIS

Slowly

Some - where the sun is shin - ing. Some-where the song birds dwell. Hush, then, thy sad re - pin - ning. God lives, and all is well. Some where, Some - where, Beau - ti - ful Isle Of Some - Where. Land of the true, where we live a - new, Beau - ti - ful Isle Of Some - where.

Battle Hymn of the Republic

By JULIA WARD HOWE and WILLIAM STEFFE

1. Mine___ eyes have seen the glo - ry of the com - ing of the Lord; He is
2. I have seen Him in the watch-fires of a hun -dred cir - cling camps; They have
3. He has sound - ed forth the trum -pet that shall nev - er call re - treat; He is
4. In the beau -ty of the lil - ies Christ was born a - cross the sea, With a

tram - pling out the vin - tage where the grapes of wrath are stored; He hath
build - ed Him an al - tar in the eve - ning dews and damps; I can
sift - ing out the hearts of men be - fore His judge -ment seat; O be
glo - ry in His bos - om that trans - fig - ures you and me; As He

loosed the fate - ful light - ning of His ter - ri - ble swift sword; His
read His right - eous sen - tence by the dim and flar - ing lamps, His
swift, my soul, to an - swer Him; be ju - bi - lant, my feet! Our
died to make men ho - ly, let us die to make men free! While

truth is march - ing on.
day is march - ing on.
God is march - ing on.
God is march - ing on.

Glo - ry! glo - ry! Hal - le -
lu - jah! Glo - ry! glo - ry! Hal - le - lu - jah!

Glo - ry! glo - ry! Hal -le - lu - jah! His truth is march-ing on.

115

Believe Me if All Those Endearing Young Charms

Believe me, if all those en-dear-ing young charms, Which I gaze on so fond-ly to-day,_____ Were to change by to-mor-row and fleet in my arms, Like_ fair-y gifts fad-ing a-way,_____ Thou would still be a-dored, As this mo-ment thou art, Let thy love-li-ness fade as it will,_____ And a-round the dear ru-in each wish of my heart, Would en-twine it-self ver-dant-ly still. _____

It is not while beauty and youth are thine own,
And thy cheeks unprofaned by a tear;
But the fervor and faith of a soul can be known,
To which time will but make thee more dear.

Oh, the heart that has truly loved never forgets,
But as truly loves on to the close
As the sunflower turns on her god when he sets
The same look that she gave when he rose.

Black is the Color of My True Love's Hair

mf Black is the col-or of my true love's___ hair, Her lips _____ are like a rose so fair, And the pret-ti-est face and the neat-est ___ hands, I love _____ the ground on which she stands.

Bill Bailey

By HUGHIE CANNON

A Bicycle Built for Two

By HARRY DACRE

Buffalo Gals

Folk Song

Lively

Buf - fa - lo gals, won't you come out to - night? Come out to - night?

Come out to - night? Buf - fa - lo gals won't you come out to - night? And

dance by the light of the moon? Dance with a doll with a

hole in her stock - ing, And her toe keeps a - knock - ing, And her

heel keeps a - rock - ing, Gon - na dance with a doll with a

hole in her stock - ing, Gon - na dance by the light of the

moon. Oh! Buf - fa - lo gals won't you come out to - night?

Come out to - night? Come out to - night? Buf - fa - lo gals won't you

Come out to - night? And dance by the light of the moon?

Blue Tail Fly

1. When I was young I used to wait
   On Massa, and hand him his plate,
   And pass the bottle when he got dry,
   And brush away the blue-tail fly.

   Jimmie crack corn and I don't care,
   Jimmie crack corn and I don't care,
   Jimmie crack corn and I don't care,
   Old Massa's gone away.

2. And when he rides in the afternoon,
   I'd follow with a hickary broom;
   The pony he was like to shy
   When bitten by a blue-tail fly.

   Jimmie crack corn etc.

3. One day he ride around the farm,
   The flies so thick that they did swarm,
   One chanced to bite him on the thigh;
   The devil take the blue-tail fly.

   Jimmie crack corn etc.

4. The pony run, he jump, he pitch,
   And threw old Massa in the ditch.
   He died and the jury pondered why;
   The verdict was the blue-tail fly.

   Jimmie crack corn etc.

5. They laid him under a 'simmon tree;
   His epitaph is there to see;
   "Beneath this stone I'm forced to lie,
   A victim of the blue-tail fly"

   Jimmie crack corn etc.

C.C. Rider

Camptown Races

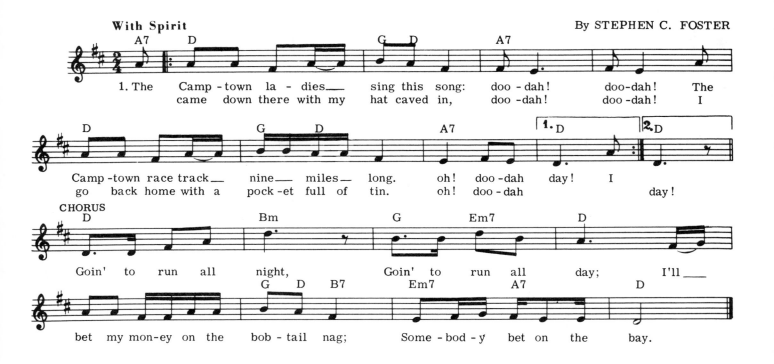

With Spirit

By STEPHEN C. FOSTER

1. The Camp-town la - dies___ sing this song: doo -dah! doo -dah! The
   came down there with my hat caved in, doo -dah! doo -dah! I

Camp -town race track___ nine___ miles___ long. oh! doo -dah day! I
go back home with a pock -et full of tin. oh! doo -dah day!

CHORUS

Goin' to run all night, Goin' to run all day; I'll___

bet my mon-ey on the bob - tail nag; Some - bod - y bet on the bay.

Careless Love

Moderato

1. Love, oh love, oh careless love,
   Love, oh love, oh careless love,
   Oh well it's love, oh love, oh careless love,
   You see what careless love has done.

2. Sorrow, sorrow to my heart,
   Sorrow, sorrow to my heart,
   Oh well, it's sorrow, sorrow to my heart,
   Since my true love and I did part.

3. Cried last night, the night before,
   Cried last night, the night before,
   Oh well, I cried last night, the night before,
   I'll cry tonight, and cry no more.

Clementine

Folk Song

Medium Waltz

In a cav-ern in a can-yon, Ex-ca-vat-ing for a mine, Dwelt a
min-er, For-ty-nin-er, And his daught-er Clem-en-tine. Oh my dar-ling, Oh my
dar-ling, Oh my dar-ling Clem-en-tine, You are lost and gone for ev-er, Dread-ful
sor-ry, Clem-en-tine. She drove duck-lings to the wat-er, Ev-'ry
morn-ing just at nine, Hit her big toe 'gainst a splin-ter Fell in-to the foam-ing brine.
Oh my dar-ling, Oh my dar-ling, Oh my dar-ling Clem-en-
tine, You are lost and gone for-ev-er, Dread-ful sor-ry, Clem-en-tine.

Deep River

Slowly

Deep river, My home is over Jordan,
Deep river, Lord, I want to cross over into camp-ground.
Lord, I am a-comin', Lord, I am a-comin',
I want to cross over into camp-ground, camp-ground, Lord!

Comin' Thro the Rye

1. 'Gin a body meet a body,
   Comin' thro' the rye,
   If a body kiss a body,
   Need a body cry?

   Ev'ry lassie has her laddie,
   Nane, they say, ha'e I,
   Yet a' the lads they smile on me,
   When comin' thro' the rye.

2. 'Gin a body meet a body,
   Comin' frae the toun,
   If a body greet a body,
   Need a body froun?

   Ev'ry lassie etc.

3. Amang the train there is a swain
   I dearly love mysel',
   But what's his name, or where's his hame,
   I dinna choose to tell.

   Ev'ry lassie etc.

Down by the Riverside

1. Gonna walk with my baby,
   Down by the riverside.   *3 times*
   Gonna talk with my baby,
   Down by the riverside.   *twice*

   Then I'll take her by the hand
   And I know she'll understand
   Just what I have to say,
   When I whisper "I love you,"
   If she says "I love you, too,"
   I'll ask her to name the day.

2. Then I'll carry my baby,
   Down by the riverside.   *3 times*
   And I'll marry my baby,
   Down by the riverside.   *twice*

   Then I'll take her etc.

Down in the Valley

1. Down in the valley, valley so low,
   In ev'ning's twilight hear that train blow.
   Hear that train blow, dear, hear that train blow,
   In ev'ning's twilight hear that train blow.

2. Roses love sunshine, violets love dew,
   Angels in heaven know I love you.
   Know I love you, dear, know I love you,
   Angels in heaven know I love you.

3. Write me a letter, send it by mail,
   Please send it care of Birmingham jail.
   Birmingham jail, dear, Birmingham jail,
   Please send it care of Birmingham jail.

4. Only one year love, feeling so blue,
   Then I'll be free love, to marry you.
   To marry you, love, to marry you,
   Then I'll be free love, to marry you.

Emperor Waltz

The Entertainer

Lyric by JOHN BRIMHALL
Music by SCOTT JOPLIN

Now the cur-tain is go-ing up, The En-ter-tain-er is tak-ing a bow; Does his dance step and sings his song, E-ven gets all the au-di-ence to sing a-long, Yes, he knows just what he must do, Knows how to bring down the house when he's through: Snap-py pat-ter and jokes, he knows what pleas-es the folks, The En-ter-tain-er, the star of the show. It was in show.

Interlude

vau-de-ville and he was on the bill With all the sing-ers, danc-ers, ac-ro-bats and clowns. There was a danc-ing bear, e-ven a dog act there And a co-me-di-an who nev-er let 'em down. But when he came on to do his fa-v'rite song He real-ly wowed 'em in the ci-ties and the towns. They came from near and far to see the vau-de-ville star, The En-ter-tain-er. Now the

124

The Foggy, Foggy Dew

1. When I was a bach'lor I lived all alone,
   And worked at the weaver's trade,
   And the only, only thing I did that was wrong
   Was to woo a fair young maid.
   I wooed her in the winter time,
   And in the summer too,
   And the only, only thing I did that was wrong
   Was to keep her from the foggy, foggy dew.

2. One night she knelt close by my side
   When I was fast asleep,
   She threw her arms around my neck,
   And then began to weep.
   She wept, she cried, she tore her hair,
   Ah me! what could I do?
   So all night long I held her in my arms,
   Just to keep her from the foggy, foggy dew.

3. Oh, I'm a bachelor, I live with my son,
   We work at the weaver's trade,
   And every single time I look into his eyes
   He reminds me of the fair young maid.
   He reminds me of the winter time,
   And of the summer too,
   And the many, many times I held her in my arms,
   Just to keep her from the foggy, foggy dew.

For He's a Jolly Good Fellow

For he's a jolly good fellow,   *3 times*
And so say all of us.   *3 times*
For he's a jolly good fellow,   *3 times*
And so say all of us.

Forty-Five Minutes from Broadway

by GEO. M. COHAN

On - ly For - ty - Five Min - utes From Broad - way, think of the chan - ges it
brings; _____ For the short time it takes, what a diff - 'rence it makes In the ways of the
peo - ple and things. _____ Oh! what a fine bunch of ru - bens,
Oh! what a gay at - mos - phere; _____ They have whisk - ers like hay, and im - ag - ine Broad -
way on - ly for - ty - five min - utes from here. _____ On - ly here. _____

Frankie and Johnnie

1. Frankie and Johnny were lovers,
   O Lordy, how they did love!
   They swore to be true to each other,
   As true as the stars above,
   He was her man, but he done her wrong.

2. Frankie went down to the corner,
   Just for a bottle of beer
   She said to the waiting bar - tender,
   "Has my Johnny been in here?
   He is my man, he'd do me no wrong".

3. "Don't want to cause you no trouble,
   Don't want to tell you no lie,
   But Johnny was in, and he left
   With a girl named Nelly Bly.
   He is your man, but he done you wrong".

4. Frankie went down to the hotel,
   Opened the door to room five,
   And there on the bed sat her Johnny,
   Making love to Nelly Bly.
   He was her man, but he done her wrong.

5. Frankie drew out her revolver,
   There were no more words to say,
   And right through his heart she shot Johnny,
   And looked at him there where he lay.
   He was her man, but he done her wrong.

6. It was the big chair for Frankie,
   Calmly she waited her Fate.
   "I wonder if I'll see my Johnny,
   Standing at the Pearly Gate?
   He was my man, tho' he done me wrong."

The Girl I Left Behind Me

TRADITIONAL

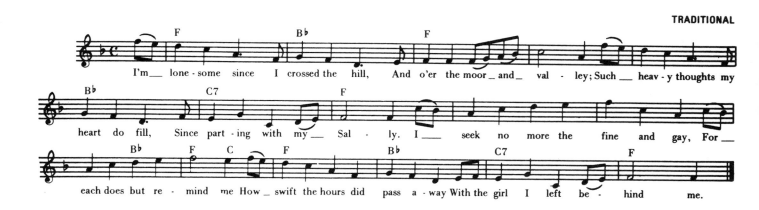

I'm__ lone-some since I crossed the hill, And o'er the moor__ and__ val - ley; Such __ heav - y thoughts my heart do fill, Since part - ing with my __ Sal - ly. I __ seek no more the fine and gay, For __ each does but re - mind me How __ swift the hours did pass a - way With the girl I left be - hind me.

Give Me that Old Time Religion

Give me that old time religion, *3 times*
It's good enough for me.

It was good for the Hebrew children, *3 times*
And it's good enough for me.

Give me that old time religion. *3 times*
It's good enough for me.

It will do when the world's on fire, *3 times*
And it's good enough for me.

Give me that old time religion, *3 times*
It's good enough for me.

Go Tell It on the Mountain

Go tell it on the mountain,
Over the hills and everywhere.
Go tell it on the mountain,
That Jesus Christ is-a born.

'Twas in a lowly manger
That Jesus Christ was born;
The Lord sent down an angel
That bright and glorious morn.

When I was a sinner,
I prayed both night and day;

I asked the Lord to help me,
And he showed me the way.

When I was a seeker,
I sought both night and day.
I asked my Lord to help me,
And He taught me to pray.

He made me a watchman
Upon the city wall;
And if I am a Christian,
I am the least of all.

Grandfather's Clock

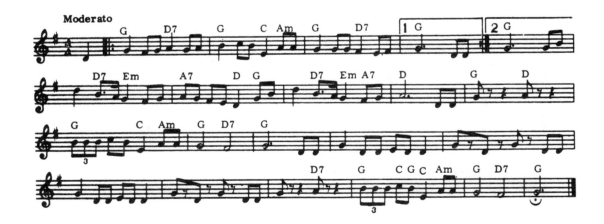

My grandfather's clock was too large for the shelf,
So it stood ninety years on the floor.
It was taller by half than the old man himself,
Though it weighed not a pennyweight more.

It was bought on the morn of the day that he was born,
And was always his treasure and pride.
But it stopped short, never to go again,
When the old man died.

Ninety years without slumbering, tick, tock, tick, tock,
His life seconds numbering, tick, tock, tick, tock,
It stopped short never to go again,
When the old man died.

Green Grow the Lilacs

1. Green grow the lilacs all sparkling with dew.
   I'm lonely, my darling, since parting with you.
   But by our next meeting I hope to prove true
   And change the green lilacs to the red, white and blue.

2. I used to have a sweetheart, but now I have none,
   Since she's gone and left me, I care not for one.
   Since she's gone and left me, contented I'll be,
   For she loves another one better than me.

3. I passed my love's window, both early and late,
   The look that she gave me, it made my heart ache.
   Oh, the look she gave me was painful to see,
   For she loves another one better than me.

4. I wrote my love letters in rosy red lines,
   She sent me an answer all twisted in twines,
   Saying, "Keep your love letters and I will keep mine,
   Just you write to your love and I'll write to mine".

   Repeat First Verse

Greensleeves

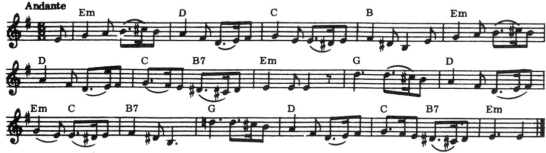

1. Alas my love you do me wrong
   To cast me off discourteously,
   And I have loved you so long,
   Delighting in your company.

   Greensleeves was all my joy,
   Greensleeves was my delight,
   Greensleeves was my heart of gold,
   And who but my lady Greensleeves.

2. Thy smock of silk both fair and white
   With gold embroidered gorgeously,
   Thy petticoat of sendal right,
   And these I bought thee gladly.

   Greensleeves etc.

3. Greensleeves, farewell adieu, adieu,
   And God I pray to prosper thee,
   For I am still thy lover true,
   Come once again and love me.

   Greensleeves etc.

Hark, the Herald Angels Sing

By CHARLES WESLEY – FELIX MENDELSSOHN

Hark! the Her - ald an - gels sing ___ "Glo - ry to the new born King,

Peace on earth and mer - cy mild, ___ God and sin - ners rec - on - ciled!"

Joy - ful all ye na - tions rise ___ Join the tri - umph of the skies, ___

With the an - gel - ic host pro - claim: Christ is ___ born in Beth - le - hem.

Hark! the Her - ald an - gels sing "Glo - ry ___ to the new born King."

Havah Nagilah

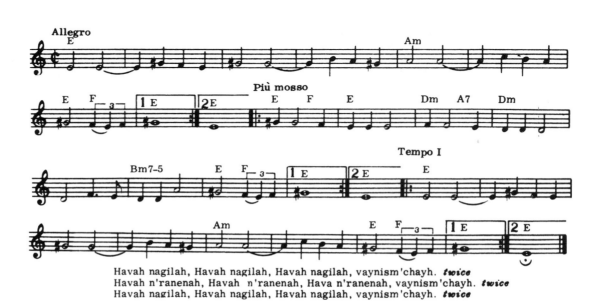

Havah nagilah, Havah nagilah, Havah nagilah, vaynism'chayh. *twice*
Havah n'ranenah, Havah n'ranenah, Hava n'ranenah, vaynism'chayh. *twice*
Havah nagilah, Havah nagilah, Havah nagilah, vaynism'chayh. *twice*

Hearts and Flowers

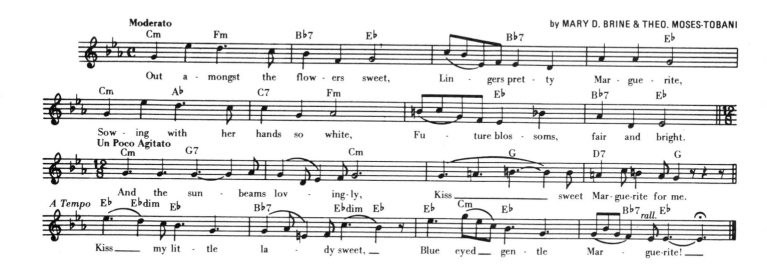

by MARY D. BRINE & THEO. MOSES-TOBANI

Moderato

Out a-mongst the flow-ers sweet, Lin-gers pret-ty Mar-gue-rite,
Sow-ing with her hands so white, Fu-ture blos-soms, fair and bright.

Un Poco Agitato

And the sun-beams lov-ing-ly, Kiss _____ sweet Mar-gue-rite for me.

A Tempo

Kiss _____ my lit-tle la-dy sweet, _____ Blue eyed _____ gen-tle Mar-gue-rite! _____

Hello! Ma Baby

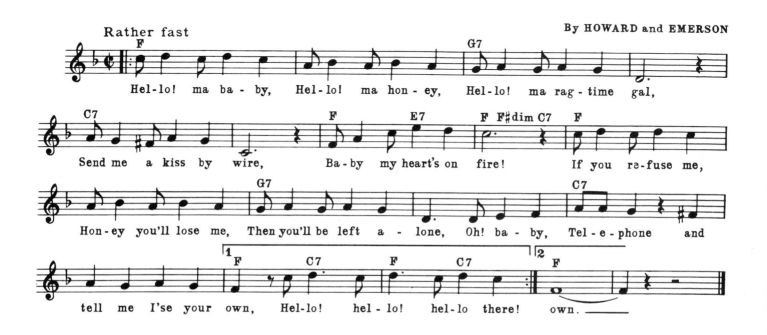

Rather fast

By HOWARD and EMERSON

Hel-lo! ma ba-by, Hel-lo! ma hon-ey, Hel-lo! ma rag-time gal,

Send me a kiss by wire, Ba-by my heart's on fire! If you re-fuse me,

Hon-ey you'll lose me, Then you'll be left a-lone, Oh! ba-by, Tel-e-phone and

tell me I'se your own, Hel-lo! hel-lo! hel-lo there! own. _____

He's Got the Whole World in His Hands

He's got the whole wide world in His hands.   *3 times*
He's got the whole world in His hands.

He's got the wind and rain in His hands,   *3 times*
He's got the whole world in His hands.

He's got the whole wide world in His hands,   *3 times*
He's got the whole world in His hands.

He's got the little baby in His hands.   *3 times*
He's got the whole world in His hands.

He's got the whole wide world in His hands.   *3 times*
He's got the whole world in His hands.

He's got both you and me in His hands,   *3 times*
He's got the whole world in His hands.

He's got the whole wide world in His hands.   *3 times*
He's got the whole world in His hands.

Home on the Range

Oh, give me a home where the buffalo roam,
And the deer and the antelope play,
Where seldom is heard a discouraging word.
And the skies are not cloudy all day.

Home, home on the range,
Where the deer and the antelope play,
Where seldom is heard a discouraging word,
And the skies are not cloudy all day.

Home, Sweet Home

Andantino

By PAYNE and BISHOP

'Mid pleasures and pal - a - ces, Though we may roam, Be it ev - er so hum - ble, there's no place like home. A charm from the sky seems to hal - low us there, Which, seek through the world, is ne'er met with else - where. Home! Home! Sweet, sweet home! There's no place like home, There's no place like home.

Hot Time in the Old Town Tonight

by JOE HAYDEN & THEO. A. METZ

Moderato

When you hear dem a bells go ding, ling ling, All join 'round And sweet - ly you must sing, and when the verse am through, In the cho - rus all join in, there'll be A Hot Time In The Old Town To - night.

House of the Rising Sun

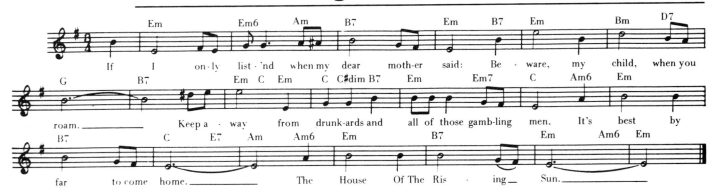

If I on-ly list-'nd when my dear moth-er said: Be-ware, my child, when you roam. _____ Keep a-way from drunk-ards and all of those gamb-ling men. It's best by far to come home. _____ The House Of The Ris-ing _____ Sun. _____

Hush Little Baby

1. Hush, little baby, don't say a word,
Papa's gonna buy you a mocking bird,
And if that mocking bird don't sing,
Papa's gonna buy you a diamond ring.

2. If that diamond ring is brass,
Papa's gonna buy you a looking glass,
And if that looking glass should crack,
Papa's gonna buy you a jumping jack.

3. If that jumping jack won't hop,
Papa's gonna buy you a lollipop,
When that lollipop is done,
Papa's gonna buy you another one.

4. If that lollipop is all eaten up,
Papa's gonna buy you a real live pup,
If that puppy dog won't bark,
Papa's gonna buy you a meadow lark.

5. If that diamond ring is glass,
Papa's gonna buy you a cup of brass,
And from that cup you'll drink your milk,
And papa's gonna dress you in the finest silk.

6. Yes, papa's gonna dress you in the finest silk,
And mama's gonna raise you
with honey and milk,
So hush, little baby, sleep safe and sound,
You're still the sweetest little babe in town.

I Gave My Love a Cherry

1. I gave my love a cherry that has no stone,
I gave my love a chicken that has no bone,
I gave my love a ring that has no end,
I gave my love a baby with no cryen.

2. How can there be a cherry that has no stone?
How can there be a chicken that has no bone?
How can there be a ring that has no end?
How can there be a baby with no cryen?

3. A cherry when it's blooming, it has no stone,
A chicken when it's piping, it has no bone,
A ring when it's rolling, it has no end,
A baby when it's sleeping has no cryen.

I'll Take You Home Again, Kathleen

I'll take you home again Kathleen,
Across the ocean wild and wide,
To where your heart has ever been
Since you became my lovely bride.

The roses all have left your cheek,
I've watched them fade away and die:
Your voice is sad whene'er you speak,
And tears bedim your lovely eyes.

Oh, I will take you back Kathleen,
To where your heart will feel no pain,
And when the fields are fresh and green,
I'll take you to your home again.

In the Good Ol' Summertime

By REN SHIELDS and GEORGE EVANS

IN THE GOOD OLD SUM - MER TIME,_____ IN THE GOOD OLD SUM - MER TIME. _____

Stroll - ing thro' the sha - dy lanes, With your ba - by mine;_____ You

hold her hand and she holds yours, And that's a ver - y good sign _____ That

she's your toot - sey woot - sey IN THE GOOD OLD SUM - MER TIME. _____

I Ride an Old Paint

1. I ride an old Paint, I lead an old Dan,
I'm a-goin' to Montana to throw the Hoolihan:
Where they water in the coulies, they feed in the draw,
Their backs are all matted, their tails are all raw.

Won't you ride around easy, ride around slow,
For the fiery and snuffy are rarin' to go.

2. Now old Bill Jones had two daughters and a song,
The one went to Denver, the other went wrong:
His wife she died in a poolroom fight,
But still he keeps singin' from morning till night.

Won't you ride around etc.

3. Now, when I die take my saddle from the wall,
Put it on my pony, lead him out of his stall;
Tie my bones to his back, turn our faces to the west,
We'll ride the prairies that we love the best.

Won't you ride around etc.

I've Been Working on the Railroad

Jeanie with the Light Brown Hair

By STEPHEN FOSTER

Jingle Bells

Traditional

John Henry

1. John Henry said to his captain:
"Captain, when you go to town,
Bring me back a nine-pound sledge hammer
And I'll drive that steel right down,
      (Lord, Lord!)
And I'll drive that steel right down."

2. John Henry said to his captain:
"After all, a man is a man,
'Fore I let that steam drill beat me,
I'll die with my hammer in my hand,
      (Lord, Lord!)
I'll die with my hammer in my hand."

3. John Henry lifted his hammer,
Drove till his hammer caught on fire,
Last words I hear John Henry say,
"A cool drink of water 'fore I die,
      (Lord, Lord!)
A cool drink of water 'fore I die".

4. Laid old John Henry on the cool ground,
Looked at him good and long;
Last words I hear his good wife say,
"My man he is dead and gone,
      (Lord, Lord!)
My man he is dead and gone"

Johnny, I Hardly Know You

When go-ing the road to sweet A-thy, hu - roo!___ Hu - roo!___ When
go-ing the road to sweet A-thy, hu - roo!___ Hu - roo!___ When___
go-ing the road to sweet A-thy, A stick in my hand and a drop in my eye, A ___
dole -ful dam- sel I heard cry, John- ny I hard- ly knew ye!

Joshua Fit the Battle of Jericho

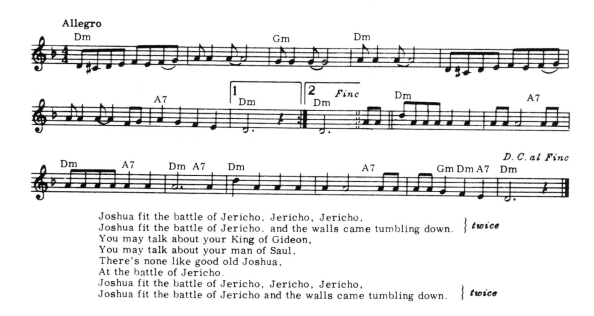

Joshua fit the battle of Jericho. Jericho, Jericho,
Joshua fit the battle of Jericho. and the walls came tumbling down. } *twice*
You may talk about your King of Gideon,
You may talk about your man of Saul.
There's none like good old Joshua,
At the battle of Jericho.
Joshua fit the battle of Jericho, Jericho, Jericho,
Joshua fit the battle of Jericho and the walls came tumbling down. } *twice*

Kum Ba Ya

Kum ba ya, O Lord, Kum ba ya,   *3 times*
O Lord, Kum ba ya!

I am waiting, Lord, Kum ba ya,   *3 times*
O Lord, Kum ba ya!

I am praying, Lord, Kum ba ya,   *3 times*
O Lord, Kum ba ya!

La Bamba

Dance La Bamba! A cousin of the samba.
Ay, ay, caramba! oh! the spell of La Bamba!
Wild and frantic and romantic!
Come, let's chance it, come, let's dance it.
Come on and dance La Bamba,
Come on and dance La Bamba,
Ariba, ariba, ariba,
Let's answer the call of the dance.
Come, let's dance to La Bamba!
Come, let's dance to La Bamba!

La Cucaracha

La Cucaracha, La Cucaracha, he's a merry little bug.
La Cucaracha, La Cucaracha, scampering across the rug.
La Cucaracha, La Cucaracha, first he will and then he won't.
La Cucaracha, La Cucaracha, now you see him, now you don't.

Londonderry Air

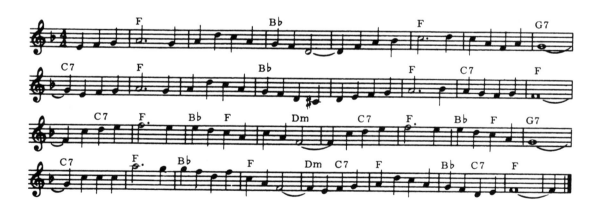

My heart still yearns for my old Londonderry home,
And for the folks who still wait there for me.
I will return to dear old Londonderry soon,
No more to roam again, my heart will ever stay.

My sweetheart there will welcome me with open arms,
And hold me close beside her evermore.
And side by side we'll keep the home fires burning bright,
In Londonderry where my heart will ever be.

Meet Me in St. Louis, Louis

By STERLING and MILLS

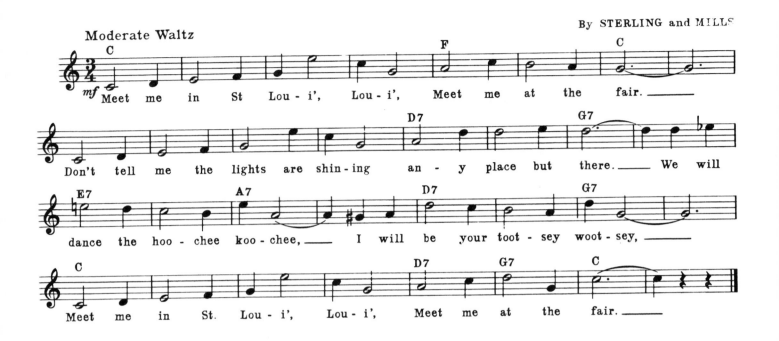

Meet me in St Lou - i', Lou - i', Meet me at the fair. ____
Don't tell me the lights are shin - ing an - y place but there. ____ We will
dance the hoo - chee koo - chee, ____ I will be your toot - sey woot - sey, ____
Meet me in St. Lou - i', Lou - i', Meet me at the fair. ____

Merry Widow Waltz

FRANZ LEHAR

Michael, Row the Boat Ashore

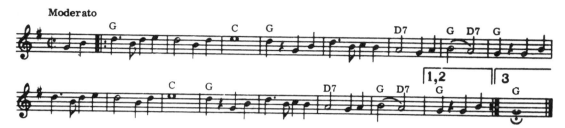

Michael, row the boat ashore, Hallelujah,
Michael, row the boat ashore, Hallelujah,

1. Tho' the river's deep and wide, Hallelujah!
   Must get to the other side, Hallelujah!

   Michael, row the boat etc.

2. Tho' the river's dark and cold, Hallelujah!
   There is fire in my soul, Hallelujah!

   Michael, row the boat etc.

3. Tho' the river's smooth and fast, Hallelujah!
   We will reach the bank at last, Hallelujah!

   Michael, row the boat etc.

My Bonnie

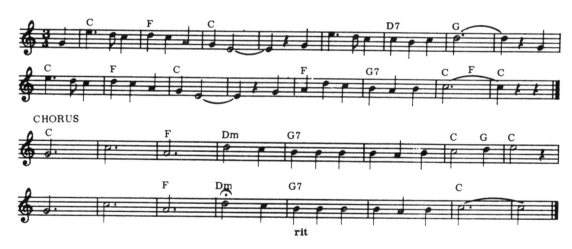

1. My Bonnie is over the ocean,
   My Bonnie is over the sea,
   My Bonnie is over the ocean,
   Oh, bring back my Bonnie to me.

   Bring back, bring back,
   Oh, bring back my Bonnie to me, to me.
   Bring back, bring back,
   Oh, bring back my Bonnie to me!

2. Oh, blow ye winds over the ocean,
   Oh, blow ye winds over the sea,
   Oh, blow ye winds over the ocean,
   And bring back my Bonnie to me.

   Bring back etc.

3. Last night as I lay on my pillow,
   Last night as I lay on my bed,
   Last night as I lay on my pillow,
   I dreamed that my Bonnie was dead.

   Bring back etc.

4. The winds have blown over the ocean,
   The winds have blown over the sea,
   The winds have blown over the ocean,
   And brought back my Bonnie to me.

   Bring back etc.

My Gal Sal

By PAUL DRESSER

Slow Waltz

They called her fri-vo-lous Sal, ___ A pe-cu-liar sort of a gal, ___ With a heart that was mel-low, An all 'round good fel-low Was my old pal. ___ Your trou-bles, sor-rows and care, ___ She was al-ways will-ing to share, ___ A wild sort of dev-il, But dead on the lev-el was My Gal Sal. ___

My Old Kentucky Home

1. The sun shines bright on the old Kentucky home,
   'Tis summer, the darkies are gay;
   The corntop's ripe and the meadow's in bloom,
   While the birds make music all the day.

2. The young folks roll on the little cabin floor,
   All merry, all happy and bright;
   By'n bye hard times come a-knocking at the door,
   Then my old Kentucky home, good-night.

3. Weep no more my lady,
   Oh, weep no more today.
   We will sing one song for the old Kentucky home,
   For my old Kentucky home far away.

144

Nowell

Traditional

Moderato

1. The first Nowell the an-gel did say Was to cer-tain poor shep-herds in fields as they lay, In fields where they lay keep-ing their sheep On a cold win-ter's night that was so deep.
2. They looked up and saw a star Shin-ing in the East be-yond them far And to the earth it gave great light And so it con-tin-ued both day and night.
3. This star drew nigh to the north-west, O'er Beth-le-hem it took its rest And there it did both stop and stay High o-ver the place where Je-sus lay.
4. Then en-tered in those wise men three, Fell rev-'rent-ly up-on their knees And of-fered there in His pre-sence Their gold and myrrh and frank-in-cense.
5. Then let us all with one ac-cord Sing prais-es to our heav-en-ly Lord That hath made heav'n and earth of naught And with His blood man-kind hath bought.

Now-ell, Now-ell, Now-ell, Now-ell, Born is the King of Is-ra-el!

Nobody Knows the Trouble I've Seen

Slowly

Nobody knows the trouble I've seen,
Nobody knows but Jesus,
Nobody knows the troubles I've seen,
Glory Hallelujah!

Sometimes I'm up, sometimes I'm down:
Oh, yes, Lord!
Sometimes I'm almost to the ground,
Oh, yes, Lord!

Although you see me goin' 'long so
Oh, yes, Lord!
I have my trials here below,
Oh, yes, Lord!

Nobody knows etc.

O Christmas Tree

Moderately

Christmas Song

O Christ-mas tree! O Christ-mas tree! Thy leaves, they are un - chang-ing. Not on - ly green when sum-mer's here, But when the win - t'ry winds ap-pear. O Christ-mas tree! O Christ-mas tree! Thy leaves, they are un - chang-ing.

O Come All Ye Faithful

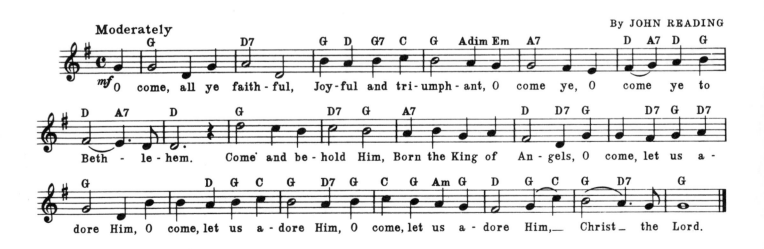

Moderately

By JOHN READING

O come, all ye faith-ful, Joy-ful and tri-umph-ant, O come ye, O come ye to Beth - le-hem. Come and be-hold Him, Born the King of An - gels, O come, let us a-dore Him, O come, let us a - dore Him, O come, let us a - dore Him,___ Christ___ the Lord.

Ode to Joy

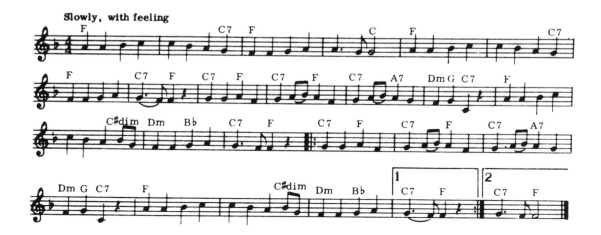

Slowly, with feeling

Sing to joy and gladness now and evermore to freedom's song.
Open up our heart's desire with love that's everlasting.
Let this magic bring together all who dwell upon the earth.
All mankind shall be together and peace shall reign upon the earth.
May this joy of brotherhood spread all through the universe.
Then the very air we breathe shall be pure and calm and gentle.

Blue the sky, and green the forest, all our children can run free
And through music bring together all who sing the Ode to Joy.

Oh Dear, What Can the Matter Be?

Allegretto

Oh dear, what can the matter be?
Dear, dear, what can the matter be?
Oh dear, what can the matter be?
Johnny's so long at the fair.

1. He promised he'd buy me a beautiful fairing,
   A gay bit of lace that the girls are all wearing,
   He promised he'd bring me a bunch of blue ribbons
   To tie up my bonnie brown hair.

   And it's oh dear, etc.

2. He promised he'd buy me a basket of posies,
   A garland of lilies, a wreath of red roses,
   A little straw hat to set off the blue ribbons
   That tie up my bonnie brown hair.

   And it's oh dear, etc.

Oh, Susanna

1. I come from Alabama wid my banjo on my knee.
   I'm gwine to Lousiana my true love for to see.

2. I had a dream the other night, when ev'rything was still:
   I tho't I saw Susanna a-comin' down the hill.

   Oh! Susanna, Oh! don't you cry for me.
   I've come from Alabama wid my banjo on my knee. } *twice*

The Old Folks at Home

'Way down upon the Swanee River,
Far, far away,
There's where my heart is turning ever,
There's where the old folks stay.
All the world is sad and dreary,
Ev'rywhere I roam;
Oh! darkies, how my heart grows weary,
Far from the old folks at home.

Oh, Them Golden Slippers

1. Oh, my gol-den slip-pers am— laid a - way 'cause I don't 'spect to wear 'em till my
2. Oh, my old ban-jo— hangs— on the wall 'cause it ain't been— tuned— since—

wed-ding day, And my long - tailed coat, that I loved— so well, I will
way last fall, But the folks all say we will have a good time, When we

wear up in the char-iot in the morn. And my long, white robe, — that I
ride— in the char-iot in the morn. There's old broth-er Ben— and—

bought last June, I'm— going— to get changed—'cause it fits too soon, And the
sis-ter Luce, They will tel - e - graph the news to Un - cle Tobac-co Juice, What a

old gray horse— that I used to drive, I will hitch him to the char-iot in the morn.
great camp meet in' there will be that day, When we ride up in the char-iot in the morn.

Oh, them gol - den slip - pers! Oh, them gol - den slip-pers! Gol - den slip-pers I'm

going to wear, be - cause they look so neat; Oh, them gol - den slip-pers! Oh, those

gol - den slip - pers! Gol - den slip - pers I'm going to wear, To walk the gol - den street.

The Old Grey Mare

Oh, the old grey mare, she ain't what she used to be,
Ain't what she used to be, ain't what she used to be,
The old grey mare, she ain't what she used to be
Many long years ago.
Many long years ago, many long years ago,
Oh, the old grey mare, she ain't what she used to be
Many long years ago.

Old MacDonald Had a Farm

Moderato

1. Old Mac Donald had a farm,
   E-I-E-I-O!
   And on this farm he had some chicks,
   E-I-E-I-O!
   With a chick, chick here and a
   chick, chick there,
   Here a chick, there a chick,
   ev'rywhere a chick, chick.
   Old Mac Donald had a farm,
   E-I E-I-O!

2. Old Mac Donald had a farm,
   E-I-E-I-O!
   And on this farm he had some ducks,
   E-I-E-I-O!
   With a quack, quack here and a
   quack, quack there,
   Here a quack, there a quack,
   ev'rywhere a quack, quack.
   Old Mac Donald had a farm,
   E-I-E-I-O!

3. Old Mac Donald had a farm,
   E-I-E-I-O!
   And on this farm he had some turkeys
   E-I-E-I-O!
   With a gobble, gobble here and a
   gobble, gobble there,
   Here a gobble, there a gobble,
   ev'ry where a gobble, gobble.
   Old Mac Donald had a farm,
   E-I-E-I-O!

4. Old Mac Donald had a farm,
   E-I-E-I-O!
   And on this farm he had some pigs,
   E-I-E-I-O!
   With an oink, oink here and an
   oink, oink there,
   Here an oink, there an oink,
   ev'rywhere an oink, oink.
   Old Mac Donald had a farm,
   E-I-E-I-O!

5. Old Mac Donald had a farm,
   E-I-E-I-O!
   And on this farm he had a Ford,
   E-I-E-I-O!
   With a rattle, rattle here and a
   rattle, rattle there,
   Here a rattle, there a rattle,
   ev'rywhere a rattle, rattle.
   Old Mac Donald had a farm,
   E-I-E-I-O!

Onward, Christian Soldiers

March tempo

On Top of Old Smokey

Over the River and Through the Woods

Over the river and thro' the woods, to grandfather's house we go.
The horse knows the way to carry the sleigh thro' the white and drifted snow.
Over the river and thro' the woods, oh how the wind does blow!
It stings the toes, and bites the nose, as over the ground we go.

Polly Wolly Doodle

1. Oh, I went down South for to see my Sal,
   Sing Polly-Wolly-Doodle all the day;
   My Sally am a spunky gal,
   Sing Polly-Wolly-Doodle all the day.

   Fare thee well, fare thee well,
   Fare thee well, my fairy fay,
   For I'm going to Louisiana, for to see my Susy-anna,
   Sing Polly-Wolly-Doodle all the day.

2. Oh, my Sal, she am a maiden fair,
   Sing Polly-Wolly-Doodle all the day:
   With laughing eyes and curly hair,
   Sing Polly-Wolly-Doodle all the day.

   Fare thee well, etc.

3. Oh, a grasshopper sittin' on a railroad track,
   Sing Polly-Wolly-Doodle all the day;
   A-pickin' his teeth wid a carpet tack,
   Sing Polly-Wolly-Doodle all the day.

   Fare thee well, etc.

4. Oh, I went to bed, but it wasn't no use,
   Sing Polly-Wolly-Doodle all the day;
   My feet stuck out for a chicken roost,
   Sing Polly-Wolly-Doodle all the day.

   Fare thee well, etc.

5. Behind de barn, down on my knees,
   Sing Polly-Wolly-Doodle all the day;
   I thought I heard that chicken sneeze,
   Sing Polly-Wolly-Doodle all the day.

   Fare thee well, etc.

6. He sneezed so hard wid de 'hoopin'-cough,
   Sing Polly-Wolly-Doodle all the day;
   He sneezed his head an' his tail right off,
   Sing Polly-Wolly-Doodle all the day.

Red River Valley

1. From this valley they say you are going,
   We will miss your bright eyes and sweet smile,
   For they say you are taking the sunshine
   That has brightened our pathway for a while.

2. You will think of the valley you're leaving,
   Oh, how lonely and sad it will be,
   Oh, think of the fond heart you are breaking,
   And the grief you are causing to me.

Rise and Shine

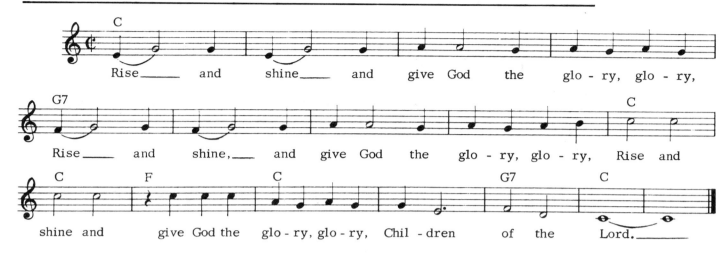

Rise____ and shine____ and give God the glo-ry, glo-ry,
Rise____ and shine,____ and give God the glo-ry, glo-ry, Rise and
shine and give God the glo-ry, glo-ry, Chil-dren of the Lord.____

The Lord said, "Noah, there's gonna be a floody, floody"...
Get your childrenn out of the muddy, muddy!"

Noah, he built him, he built him an arky, arky...
Made it out of hickory barky, barky...

The animals, they came, they came by twosy, twosy...
Elephants and kangaroosy, roosy...

It rained and rained for forty daysy, daysy...
Drove the animals nearly crazy, crazy...

The sun came out and dried up the landy , landy...
Everyone felt fine and dandy...

Repeat verse one

Rock-A-My Soul

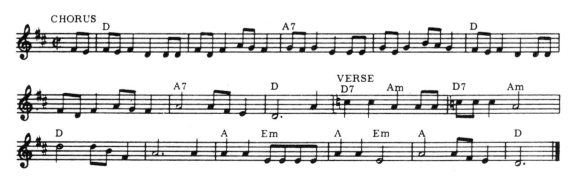

Oh, a-rocka my soul in the bosom of Abraham,
Rocka my soul in the bosom of Abraham,
Rocka my soul in the bosom of Abraham,
Oh, rocka my soul.

1. When I went down in the valley to pray,
   Oh rocka my soul.
   I got so happy that I stayed all day,
   Oh rocka my soul.

Oh, a-rocka my soul etc.

2. When I was a mourner just like you,
   Oh rocka my soul,
   I mourned and I mourned till I came through,
   Oh rocka my soul.

Rock Island Line

1. Oh the Rock Island line it's a mighty good road,
   The Rock Island line she's the road to ride,
   Yes the Rock Island line it's a mighty good road
   If you want to ride it got to ride it like you find it
   Get your ticket at the station for the Rock Island line.

   Well I may be right, I may be wrong,
   I know you're gonna miss me when I'm gone.

   Oh the Rock Island line etc.

2. A, B, C, double X, Y, Zee,
   The cat's in the cupboard, but he don't see me.

3. The engineer cried just before he died,
   There are two more drinks I would like to try,
   The doctor said what could they be,
   A hot cup of coffee and a cold glass of tea.

St. James Infirmary

I went down to the St. James Infirmary;
To see my baby there,
She was lyin' on a long white table,
So sweet, so cool, so fair.

Went up to see the doctor,
"She's very low," he said;
Went back to see my baby;
Good God! She's lyin' there dead.

I went down to old Joe's barroom,
On the corner by the square;
They were servin' the drinks as usual,
And the usual crowd was there.

On my left stood old Joe McKennedy,
And his eyes were bloodshot red;
He turned to the crowd around him,
These are the words he said:

Let her go, let her go, God bless her;
Wherever she may be;
She may search this wide world over
An' never find a better man than me.

Oh, when I die, please bury me
In my high-top Stetson hat;
Put a twenty-dollar gold piece on my watch chain
So my friends'll know I died standin' pat.

Get six gamblers to carry my coffin,
Six chorus girls to sing me a song,
Put a twenty-piece jazz band on my tail gate
To raise Hell as we go along.

Now that's the end of my story;
Let's have another round of booze;
And if anyone should ask you, just tell them
I've got the St. James Infirmary blues.

154   (repeat fifth verse)

Santa Lucia

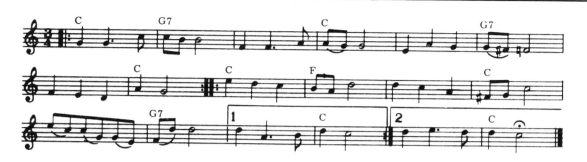

1. Now 'neath the silver moon
   Ocean is glowing,
   O'er the calm billow
   Soft winds are blowing.

2. Here balmy breezes blow,
   Pure joys invite us,
   And as we gently row,
   All things delight us.

   Hark how the sailor's cry
   Joyously echoes nigh;
   Santa Lucia! Santa Lucia!

   Home of fair poesy,
   Realm of pure harmony,
   Santa Lucia! Santa Lucia!

Scarborough Fair

2. Have her make me a cambric shirt.
   Parsley, sage, rosemary and thyme.
   Without a seam or fine needle work.
   And then she'll be a true love of mine.

4. If she tells me she can't I'll reply.
   Parsley, sage, rosemary and thyme.
   Let me know that at least she will try.
   And then she'll be a true love of mine.

The Sidewalks of New York

By CHARLES B. LAWLOR and JAMES W. BLAKE

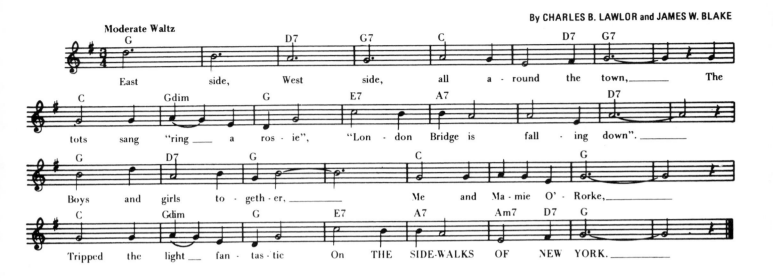

Moderate Waltz

East side, West side, all a - round the town,_____ The tots sang "ring ____ a ros - ie", "Lon - don Bridge is fall - ing down"._____ Boys and girls to - geth - er,_____ Me and Ma - mie O' - Rorke,_____ Tripped the light ___ fan - tas - tic On THE SIDE-WALKS OF NEW YORK._____

Silent Night

By MOHR and GRUBER

Slowly

Si - lent night, Ho - ly night! All is calm, All is bright 'Round yon vir - gin Moth - er and Child! Ho - ly in - fant, so ten - der and mild, Sleep in heav - en - ly peace,_____ Sleep in heav - en - ly peace._____

Silver Threads Among the Gold

by EBEN E. REXFORD & HART P. DANKS

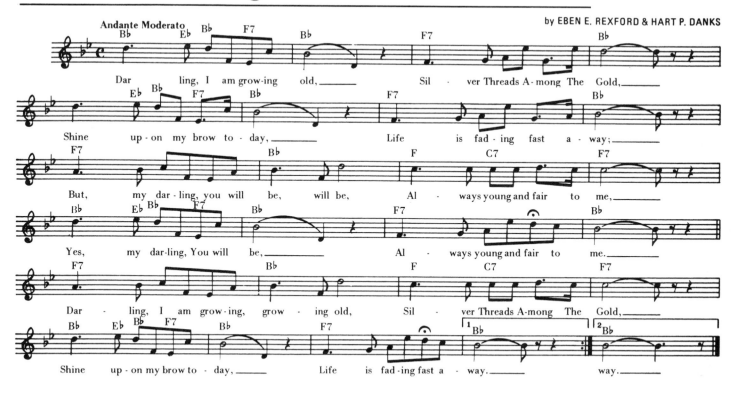

Simple Gifts

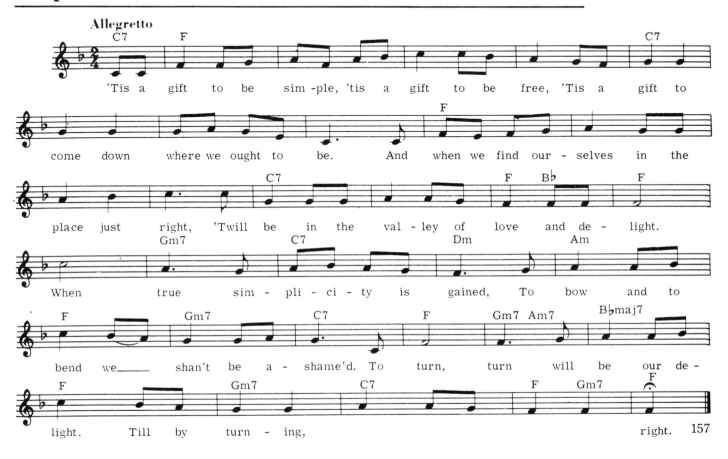

Star Spangled Banner

By FRANCIS SCOTT KEY

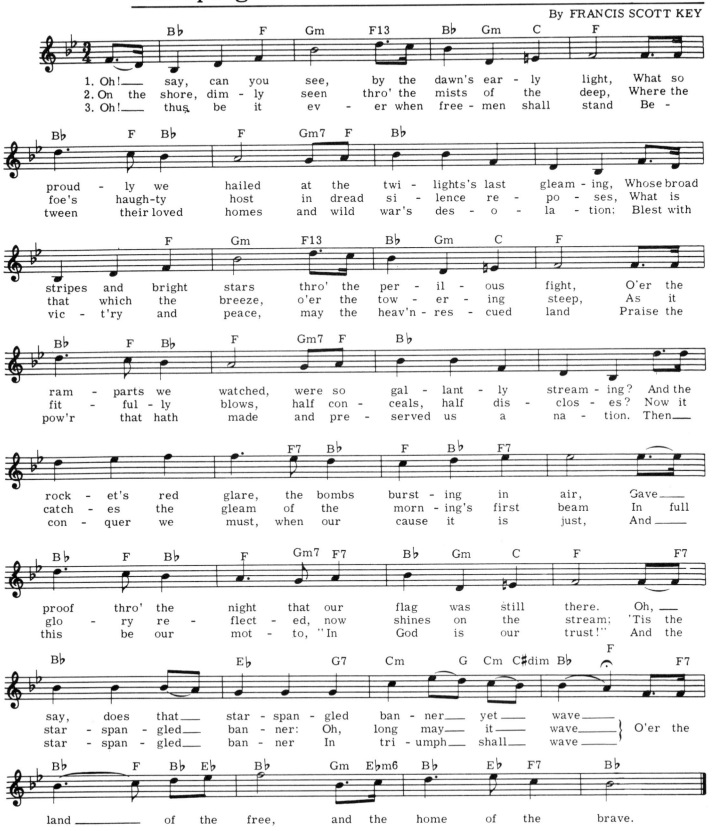

Sweet Betsy from Pike

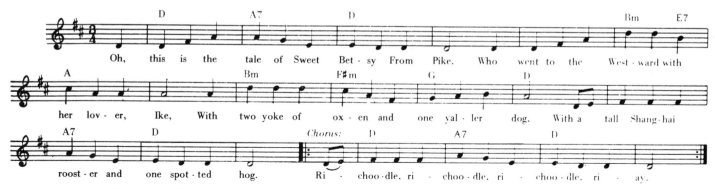

Oh, this is the tale of Sweet Bet-sy From Pike. Who went to the West-ward with her lov-er, Ike, With two yoke of ox-en and one yal-ler dog. With a tall Shang-hai roost-er and one spot-ted hog.

Chorus: Ri - choo-dle, ri - choo-dle, ri - choo-dle, ri - ay.

2. The Shanghai ran off and their cattle all died;
   That morning their last piece of bacon was fried.
   Poor Ike was discouraged and Betsy was mad:
   The yaller dog drooped and looked woefully sad.
   (Chorus)

3. They doggedly climbed up a very high hill
   And looked down with wonder on old Placerville.
   Ike smiled when he said, "Now we don't have to roam.
   California, sweet Betsy, will be our new home."
   (Chorus)

Swing Low, Sweet Chariot

Swing low, sweet char-i-ot,___ Com-in' for to car-ry me home, Swing___ low, sweet char-i-ot,___ Com-in' for to car-ry me home.___

1. I look'd o-ver Jor-dan and what did I see?___ Come-in' for to car-ry me home; Tell band___ of an-gels com-in' af-ter me,___ Com-in' for to car-ry me home.

2. If you___ get there___ be-for___ I do;___ home. all___ my friends I'm com-in'___ too,___

This Train Is Bound for Glory

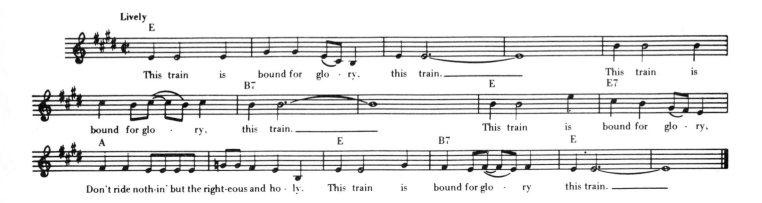

Don't ride noth-in' but the right-eous and ho - ly. This train is bound for glo - ry this train. _____

2. This train don't carry no gamblers. this train.
   This train don't carry no gamblers. this train.
   This train don't carry no gamblers.
   No crap shooters. no midnight ramblers.
   This train don't carry no gamblers. this train.

3. This train don't carry no jokers, this train.
   This train don't carry no jokers, this train.
   This train don't carry no jokers.
   Hightoned women. no cigar smokers.
   This train don't carry no jokers, well this train.

Toyland

By MacDONOUGH and HERBERT

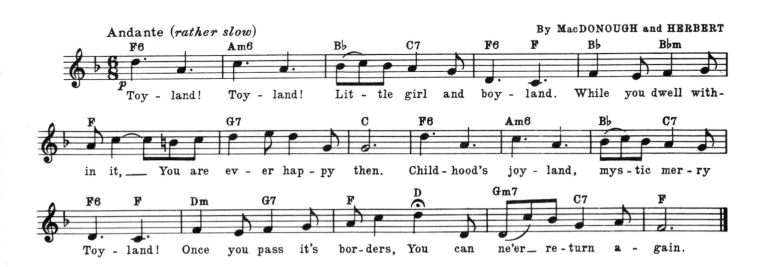

Twelve Days of Christmas

7 swans a-swimming (DS 6 to Fine)
8 maids a-milking (DS 7 to Fine)
9 ladies dancing (DS 8 to Fine)
10 lords a-leaping (9 &c)
11 pipers piping (10 &c)
12 drummers drumming
(11th day to Fine)

Under the Bamboo Tree

By BOB COLE

If you lak - a - me, lak I lak - a - you And we lak - a both the same, I lak - a say, this ver - y day, I lak - a - change your name; 'Cause I love - a - you and love - a - you true And if you - a love - a - me. One live as two, two live as one Un - der The Bam - boo Tree.

Vilia

By FRANZ LEHAR

Vi - lia, oh Vi - lia, I love you, I do! I pray that you'll say that you love me too. Vi - lia, oh Vi - lia, my dar - ling, my own, My love is yours, yours a - lone. Vi - lia, oh Vi - lia, I'm lone - ly and blue, Come to my arms, make my dreams all come true. All through the night how I sigh, how I pine: Vi - lia, dear Vi - lia, be mine.

A Wandering Minstrel

W. S. Gilbert
Sir Arthur Sullivan

A wan-d'ring min-strel I,	A thing of shreds____ and patch-es,
of bal-lads, songs and snatch-es,	And dream-y lull-a-by!
My cat-a-louge is long,	Thro' ev-'ry pas-sion rang-ing,
And to your hu-mours chang-ing	I tune__ my sup-ple song! ____
I tune__ my sup - - - ple song.____	

What Shall We Do with a Drunken Sailor?

1. What shall we do with the drunken sailor,   *3 times*
    Early in the morning.

    Hoo-ray up she rises,   *3 times*
    Early in the morning.

2. Put him in the long boat 'til he's sober,   *3 times*
    Early in the morning.

    Hoo-ray etc.

We Three Kings of Orient Are

By JOHN H. HOPKINS

We three Kings of O-ri-ent are, Bear-ing gifts to tra-verse a-far, Field and foun-tain, moor and moun-tain, fol-low-ing yon-der star. Oh! Star of won-der, Star of night, Star with roy-al beau-ty bright, West-ward lead-ing, still pro-ceed-ing, Guide us to thy per-fect light.

When You Were Sweet Sixteen

By JAMES THORNTON

I love you as I nev-er loved be-fore, Since first I met you on the vil-lage green. Come to me or my dream of love is o'er. I love you as I loved you, When you were sweet, when you were sweet six-teen. I -teen.

When You and I Were Young, Maggie

By JAMES BUTTERFIELD

I wan - dered to - day to the hill, Mag - gie, To watch the scene be - low, _____ The creek and the creak - ing old mill, Mag - gie, As we used to long a - go. _____ The green grove is gone from the hill, Mag - gie, Where first the dai - sies _____ sprung, _____ And the creak - ing old mill is _____ still, Mag - gie, Since you and _ I were _ young. I young. _____

You Tell Me Your Dream

By DANIELS, RICE and BROWN

You had a dream dear, I had one too. _____ I know mine's best, 'cause it was of you. Come sweet - heart tell me, Now is the time. _____ You tell me your dream, I'll tell _ you mine. _____

Yankee Doodle Boy

By GEORGE M. COHAN